Days of Grace

Raymond Chapman is Emeritus Professor of English in the University of London and a non-stipendiary priest in the Diocese of Southwark. He is a Vice-Chairman of the Prayer Book Society and is the author of numerous literary and religious titles.

Books by Raymond Chapman available from the Canterbury Press:

Days of Grace

*A forty-day journey
with Jesus*

Raymond Chapman

CANTERBURY
PRESS
Norwich

© Raymond Chapman 1999

First published in 1999 by The Canterbury Press Norwich
(a publishing imprint of Hymns Ancient & Modern Limited
a registered charity)
St Mary's Works, St Mary's Plain
Norwich, Norfolk, NR3 3BH

British Library Cataloguing in Publication Data

A catalogue record for this book is available
from the British Library

ISBN 1-85311-328-X

Typeset by Rowland Phototypesetting Ltd,
Bury St Edmunds, Suffolk
and printed in Great Britain by
Biddles Ltd, Guildford and King's Lynn

Contents

Introduction

The traditional practice of keeping a period of forty days before Easter as a time of fasting and penance has made many people associate Lent mainly with self-denial or 'giving up something'. To abstain from some pleasure which is permissible in itself is a valuable means of discipline and of strengthening the will to keep us strong in the Christian way. It is not, however, the whole purpose of Lent, and should accompany the more important resolution to offer extra devotion, in both private prayer and corporate worship. It is a time to consider our sins, to repent and seek to do better. It is a time to reflect on our spiritual state and our responses to God's calling to each one of us.

The devotions which follow are set out for each day of Lent, excluding the Sundays, which are not counted within the forty days. They are centred mainly on five themes which are prominent in the Bible and can focus our thoughts and prayers. Over five weeks, we consider Journeys, Mountains, Light, Food and Healing. Each of these helps us to think about the life of faith as we pass through this world. They are taken with biblical passages in which they are significant and which give us images to apply to our own situations.

In the first four days of Lent, we prepare by

reflecting about our share in the condition of humanity, as it stands under the rule of God both in its failures and in its hopes. In Holy Week the five themes are drawn into a contemplation of the Passion in which Lent finds its climax and its end.

The devotions for each day are arranged after the same pattern:

A passage from the Bible, sometimes abridged from the full account, to give the central message. Having these extracts within the book may be helpful to those who find it easier to make their devotions when travelling or away from the resources of their own home.

A commentary to give some background and suggest ideas arising from the passage.

A meditation, using the passage imaginatively to connect it with the readers' own experiences and to respond to what it seems to be saying to them.

Questions for reflection on related matters of penitence and thanksgiving.

Further reflections and prayers to help a resolution arising from meditation.

A short phrase to be remembered and repeated during the day, frequently returning the mind to what has been learned.

As with all our prayers, the ideal is to find a set period, as early as possible in the day, for the additional daily devotions of Lent. But none should be discouraged by the difficulties of a busy life that demands a more flexible approach. Anxiety and haste are the enemies of prayer, and it is better to give a few shorter times with full attention than to be going through the whole exercise with an eye on the clock.

Lent is a solemn time, but it is not meant to be a miserable one. Sorrow for our sins and for the suffering of our Lord are, in God's mercy, a means of progress in the joyful and richer life of faith. We may keep before us one of the most comforting and encouraging sayings of Jesus: 'I came that they may have life, and have it more abundantly' (John 10:10).

Biblical passages are from the New Revised Standard Version. In extracts from other sources the language and usage of the original have been preserved.

Week 1: Preparation

In this first short week of Lent, we prepare for the explorations that we shall make into some images of God's revelation. We consider who we are, our identity as members of the human race which he created to live in this world. We recognize that we have all, individually and collectively, fallen away from the loving obedience that was his desire for us. We think of the Passion, which restored us and which is the focus of our devotions at this time. We try to discern his will for us, and pray to be guided in all that we offer this Lent.

Week 1: Ash Wednesday

Who are we?
Genesis 1:26–8, 31

Then God said, 'Let us make humankind in our image, according to our likeness; and let them have dominion over the fish of the sea, and over the birds of the air, and over the cattle, and over all the wild animals of the earth, and over every creeping thing that creeps upon the earth. So God created humankind in his image, in the image of God he created them, male and female he created them. God blessed them, and God saw everything that he had made, and indeed, it was very good.

What God made was good. How could it be otherwise, since its source was his own infinite goodness and love? At this time above all others in the year, we acknowledge our sins and turn back in repentance. We cannot understand the horror of sin unless we see it as an offence against God, who has made all things well. People often say of some wrong behaviour, 'It's only natural.' Sin is not natural; it is a denial of our true human nature. Being made in the image of God does not mean that we think of God as an all-powerful being, but that he has made us to share his perfection. In our Lent devotions we are not trying to placate an angry God but to come back to the loving God who is reaching out and calling us to become what we were created to be.

Rest in silence and feel the love of God who made you as part of his perfect creation. Think of something that gives you great delight and a sense of God's presence: a scene of natural beauty, a painting, a piece of music or a loved human being. Know that God loves you with an intensity far more than any delight that you can feel in this world. He loves you as you are, knowing the depths of your being, and offers you his love to restore his image in you. See this Lent as a way of returning to him. Picture yourself among a great multitude of Christians who are on their way back to original righteousness.

Do I really believe that goodness is natural and sin unnatural? Do I regard perfect obedience to the will of God as a constraint on my personal freedom or as a fulfilment of my true self?

Thank God for life and for his loving care up to this day. Rejoice that you are allowed and enabled to come to him in penitence and resolution this Lent.

Thus, when all things had been settled with a wonderful arrangement, he determined to prepare for Himself an eternal kingdom, and to create innumerable souls, on whom he might bestow immortality. Then He made for Himself a figure endowed with perception and intelligence, that is, after the likeness of His own image, than which nothing can be more perfect.

Lactantius

Grant, we beseech thee, O Lord, that by the observance of this Lent we may advance in the knowledge of the mystery of Christ, and show forth his mind in conduct worthy of our calling; through Jesus Christ our Lord.

Gelasian Sacramentary

*

Almighty Father, creator and sustainer of all, guide me to make a good resolve for this season and give me grace to keep it. May I always remember the loving purpose that made all things good and honour the divine image in myself and in all people.

God saw all that he had made, and it was very good.

Week 1: Thursday

What have we become?
Genesis 2:16–17; 3:4–6, 23–4

The Lord God commanded the man, 'You may freely eat of every tree of the garden; but of the tree of the knowledge of good and evil you shall not eat, for in the day that you eat of it you shall die.' But the serpent said to the woman, 'You will not die, for God knows that when you eat of it your eyes will be opened, and you will be like God, knowing good and evil.' So when the woman saw that the tree was good for food, and that it was a delight to the eyes, and that the tree was to be desired to make one wise, she took of the fruit and ate; and she also gave some to her husband, and he ate. Therefore the Lord God sent him forth from the garden of Eden, to till the ground from which he was taken. He drove out the man; and at the east of the garden of Eden he placed the cherubim, and a sword flaming and turning to guard the way to the tree of life.

❖

The story of Adam and Eve eating the forbidden fruit and being cast out of the Garden of Eden is familiar even to people who know little of the

Bible. It has become a theme for light remarks about temptation, even for jokes in cartoons. To eat something you have been told not to eat seems such a little fault. But the story is a way of telling the terrible truth that human beings, made in the image of God, disobeyed him. They misused the divine power of free choice which he had given them. Those whom he had made to be most like him, to live happily and care for his created world, were those who rebelled against him. This is the 'original sin' which is not just the action of some distant ancestor but the damage to our humanity that causes us so easily to turn away from God and follow our own ways. We still give in to the temptation of superficial pleasure and immediate satisfaction.

Sin continually spoils what is good. Imagine a fine picture almost hidden by grime; a statue hacked away until its proportions are lost; a beautiful garden torn up and vandalized. That is what we have done to our souls through sin. Remember the misery that you have felt after hurting someone you really love, perhaps one of the saddest experiences that we know in this life. That is only a little way towards what we should feel about sin which offends against God. Yet he loves you still: accept the love and the sorrow together.

Am I sorry only because I feel that my good image of myself is damaged? Do embarrassment and the good opinion of others matter most when I know

I have done wrong? Can I truly say, 'O my God, I am very sorry for having sinned against YOU'?

Be thankful that sorrow for sin is the beginning of the way back. Praise God who has not left us in our fallen state without the conscience that desires good above evil.

❖

If you occasionally lapse into sin, do not lose heart and cease trying to advance, for God will draw good even out of our fall. By the blood which our Lord shed for us, I beg those already started on the right path not to let the combat turn them back from it.

St Teresa of Avila

Blessed Lord, who wast tempted in all things like as we are, have mercy on our frailty. Out of weakness give us strength. Grant to us thy fear, that we may fear thee only. Support us in time of temptation. Embolden us in the time of danger. Help us to do thy work with good courage, and to continue thy faithful soldiers and servants to our life's end; through Jesus Christ our Lord.

B. F. Westcott

*L*oving Father, I come in my weakness, my fail-ures, my frequent sins. Grant that in this Lent I shall find the spirit of true repentance, a desire to do better, and grace to live obediently according to the faith that I profess.

I acknowledge my faults and never forget my sin.

Week 1: Friday

What has God done for us?
Romans 5:12, 15–17

Sin came into the world through one man, and death came through sin, and so death spread to all because all have sinned. But the free gift was not like the trespass. For if the many died through the one man's trespass, much more surely have the grace of God and the free gift of the one man, Jesus Christ, abounded for the many. And the free gift is not like the effect of the one man's sin. For the judgement following the trespass brought condemnation, but the free gift following many trespasses brings justification. If, because of the one man's trespass, death exercised dominion through that one, much more surely will those who receive the abundance of grace and the free gift of righteousness exercise dominion in life through the one man, Jesus Christ.

❖

Here is the heart of the Christian mystery, the foundation and strength of our devotions through Lent and at all times. What was lost by human disobedience has been restored by human obedience taken into the majesty of God himself. We are forgiven not by our efforts to make amends to God for sin, but by love freely given to those who have offended him and marred his perfect creation. The new creation is even more wonderful than the first, because God has now shared our human condition, even to the death which it brought into the world. We cannot grasp the depth of the Atonement. In his play *Measure for Measure*, Shakespeare gives it fine expression. Isabella is pleading for her brother, condemned to death, and is told 'Your brother's life is forfeit to the law.' She replies,

Why, all the souls that were were forfeit once
And he that might the vantage best have took
Found out the remedy.

Think of some change from trouble to relief, from sadness to joy. It may be light from darkness; release from a locked room; receiving back a precious thing that has been lost; love restored after estrangement; health after sickness. Remember all through this Lent that your penitence, your devotions, your self-denial, are acceptable to God because he has received you back and made you whole.

Do I really accept what God has done for me, or do I think that my own efforts can make me free from sin? Or do I think that, because Christ died

for me, I do not need to make any effort at all?
Ask for grace to avoid these two ways of error.

Thank God for new life in Christ. Resolve always
to begin your prayers by praising him for himself
and his great love.

⋘◆⋙

Christ is the realised idea of our humanity.
He is God's idea of Man completed. There
is every difference between the ideal and the
actual – between what man aims to be and what
he is; a difference between the race as it is, and
the race as it existed in God's creative idea when
he pronounced it very good.

F. W. Robertson

O my Love, I cannot love thee without desir-
ing above all things to be like my Beloved.
O give me grace to tread in thy steps and conform me to thy divine image, that the more I
grow like thee, the more I may love thee, and
the more I may be loved by thee.

Bishop Thomas Ken

O our Saviour!
Thou who hast loved us, make us to love
thee,
Thou who hast sought us, make us to seek thee,
Thou who, when lost, didst find us,

be thou thyself the way, that we may find thee
and be found in thee, our only hope and our
everlasting joy.

E. B. Pusey

*

*B*lessed Christ, whose loving obedience overcame the disobedience of our race, and who
restored the image that had been lost through sin,
be my example, my guide and my strength through
this Lent and for all my life.

Christ died so that I might live.

Week 1: Saturday

What does God want us to do?
John 15:12–17

This is my commandment, that you love one another as I have loved you. No one has greater love than this, to lay down one's life for one's friends. You are my friends if you do what I command you. I do not call you servants any longer, because the servant does not know what the master is doing; but I have called you friends, because I have made known to you everything that I have heard from my Father. You did not choose me, but I chose you. And I appointed you to go and bear fruit, fruit that will last, so that the Father will give you whatever you ask him in my name. I am giving you these commands so that you may love one another.

The Prophet Micah gave a clear call to righteousness: 'What does the Lord require of you but to do justice, and to love kindness, and to walk humbly with your God?' (6:8). This is fine: but we know that wanting to be good is not enough. The sin which mars God's image is too strong for our unaided efforts. We are empowered by the sacrifice of Christ on the Cross, through the Holy Spirit which he promised to his disciples. We have a new freedom, not to live selfishly following our worst nature, but to live as we were meant to live, images of God restored. We are to obey the commands of our Lord, and to prove our love of God by love for others. The Greek text in this passage has the word *agape*: the same that St Paul uses in his great hymn to love (1 Corinthians 13). It is love that is absolute, not responding to worthiness in its object but seeking to imitate the unbounded love of God.

Imagine yourself among the disciples on the eve of the Passion. Your beloved Master has said that he is going away. You hear these words of comfort and instruction, and think that they may be the last teaching you will have from him. How eagerly you would listen, and resolve to obey. You will soon fail, desert him and leave him to be killed. But you will be received back and given new strength. Is not that how you have often treated him, and he has restored you? Go into the coming six weeks in that strength.

Do I hear and read the Bible too casually because its words are familiar? Do I really believe that it is addressed to me, in my own situation? Do I know that I too am a disciple?

Thank God for calling you into the devotions of this Lent. Be joyful in your heart, even as you sorrow for your sins and the sufferings of our Lord.

Our Lord does not care so much for the importance of our works as for the love with which they are done.

St Teresa of Avila

Lord, I give and offer up unto thee myself and all that is mine, actions and words, repose and silence; only do thou preserve and guide me, and direct my hand and tongue to things that are acceptable to thee, and withdraw me from anything from which it were better to abstain, by and for the sake of Jesus Christ our Lord.

William Laud

O God Almighty, by whom and before whom we are all brethren: grant us so truly to love one another, that evidently and beyond all doubt we may love thee; through Jesus Christ thy Son, our Lord and brother.

Christina Rossetti

*

Ah, blessed Lord, I wish I knew how I might best love you and please you, and that my love were as sweet to you as yours is to me.

Margery Kempe

Love one another, as I have loved you.

Week 2: Journeys

The Bible is full of movement: journeys of a few hours or of many years, journeys taken at the command of God, journeys to escape from danger, journeys to begin a new phase of life. The image of human life as a journey from birth to death is strong and meaningful. Like travellers on the road, we meet new people, see new places and move towards our destination. Sometimes the road is smooth and easy, sometimes we labour to gain a short distance. Sometimes we seem to remain for long in the same place, and at other times we move quickly. As we make our journey this Lent, we can look at a few of the Bible stories of journeys and relate them to our own way forward. Are we progressing in our spiritual growth, or have we stopped too long at a comfortable place and feel no inclination to move on?

Week 2: Monday

Journey into the Unknown
Genesis 12:1–4

Now the Lord said to Abram, 'Go from your country and your kindred and your father's house to the land that I will show you. I will make of you a great nation, and I will bless you, and make your name great, so that you will be a blessing. I will bless those who bless you, and the one who curses you I will curse, and in you all the families of the earth shall be blessed.' So Abram went, as the Lord had told him, and Lot went with him. Abram was seventy-five years old when he departed from Haran.

❖

Abram is the first to be told of God's special purpose for humanity. He is the supreme patriarch, from whom would come the chosen people of Israel, the preparation for the coming of God as Man. (The name 'Abraham', given to him later, means 'Father of a multitude'.) The beginning of his story is a call to go out from his native place to an unknown land to which God will lead him. His immediate obedience required great faith and courage, not only to leave all that he knew but to take his family into the many perils of travel in the ancient world. Today we seldom start on a journey without knowing our destination, but every day we are continuing the journey of life without certain knowledge of the future. The Bible reminds us, 'Do not boast about tomorrow, for you do not know what a day may bring' (Proverbs 27:1). If we seek God's guidance, we shall go on our way with confidence, sure that our direction is right even though the next stage is not yet revealed.

Step out into Lent with the trust that Abram showed when he walked away from Haran to follow God's calling. Try to imagine how he felt when, already an old man, he was told to leave everything and begin a journey to a strange land. Seek the faith which made him sure that God would fulfil his promise, the faith that sustained him through many years of journeying and perplexity. Be open to the guidance of God, not seeking after certainty but prepared to serve him as he wills, knowing that his purposes are good.

Do I really trust God, or do I want him to confirm me in the old, familiar ways? Do I want this Lent to bring me closer to him and not to satisfy my own feelings? Am I already resenting the little demands of my Lent rule? Ask for true obedience, without self-will.

Do I value the love that has brought me to this time of life? Do I acknowledge the many ways in

which I have been helped and guided? Give thanks
for the many blessings of the journey to this day.

⟨⟨◇⟩⟩

My God, I pray that I may so love and trust
thee that I may rejoice in thee. And if I
may not do so fully in this life, let me go steadily
on to the day when I come to that fullness. Let
me receive that which thou didst promise
through thy truth, that my joy may be full.

St Anselm

*

*May Christ be my companion and my guide,
through this season and through all my life.
May I follow his example to be firm in my resol-
utions, faithful in my devotions, and loving in my
dealings with others, and may I find in him assurance that whether the way is hard or easy, it is the
way of salvation and eternal life.*

**Praise God for the past and trust him for the
future.**

Week 2: Tuesday

Journey into the Wilderness
Exodus 6:2, 6–8

God spoke to Moses and said to him, 'Say to the Israelites, "I am the Lord, and I will free you from the burdens of the Egyptians and deliver you from slavery to them. I will redeem you with an outstretched arm and with mighty acts of judgement. I will take you as my people, and I will be your God. You shall know that I am the Lord your God, who has freed you from the burdens of the Egyptians. I will bring you into the land that I swore to give to Abraham, Isaac and Jacob; I will give it to you as a possession. I am the Lord."'

The Exodus from Egypt was remembered in the religion of Israel as the greatest sign of God's care for his people. He led them through the wilderness for forty years, going before them under the sign of cloud by day and fire by night. Their journey began with a miraculous crossing of the Red Sea and ended with crossing the River Jordan into the Promised Land. It was in the wilderness journey that they received the Law through Moses, overcame many enemies and experienced many examples of God's loving care. Yet they often grumbled against him and longed for the familiar daily routine of the slavery from which he had led them. In later years, the Prophets sometimes condemned the Israelites for becoming soft and complacent in the settled life of the towns, and contrasted it with what by that time seemed the purity of the wilderness.

Think of the Children of Israel going out in families, with all the possessions they could carry, into a strange, perilous world. Imagine the vast emptiness, the pitiless sun by day and the cold of unprotected desert by night. They learned to depend on God alone for their survival. Consider how you depend on him for your very existence, for preservation to this moment and for all future expectation. In the silence of prayer, be alone with him in the desert places of the soul that knows its need, and feel the love that fills what seems to be emptiness.

When my journey towards God leads me into strange places, do I still hold fast to my trust in his guiding? When days are long and weary, do I still praise him for all that he is?

Thank God for making you understand that he alone is sufficient for you. Thank him for saving you from the danger of complacency in too much comfort.

Thou are the Way –
  Hadst thou been nothing but the goal
    I cannot say
If thou hadst ever met my soul.

    I cannot see –
I, child of process – if there lies
    An end for me
Full of repose, full of replies.

    I'll not reproach
The road that winds, my feet that err.
    Access, Approach,
Art thou, Time, Way and Wayfarer.
                              Alice Meynell

*

*Lord of the wilderness, be close to me in the
dry and barren times and keep me faithful in
the times of ease. Freed by grace from the slavery
of sin, let me never trust in my own strength or
think I deserve reward for any merit, but rejoice
in the love that keeps my feet from wandering and
will bring me to the promised land of eternal life.*

**Lead me on, Lord, by day and night, until the
journey ends.**

Week 2: Wednesday

Journey of Disobedience
Jonah 1, part of verses 1–17

The word of the Lord came to Jonah son of Amittai, saying, 'Go at once to Nineveh, that great city, and cry out against it; for their wickedness has come up before me.' But Jonah set out to flee to Tarshish from the presence of the Lord. He went down to Joppa and found a ship going to Tarshish. But the Lord hurled a great wind upon the sea, and such a mighty storm came upon the sea that the ship threatened to break up. The sailors said to one another, 'Come, let us cast lots, so that we may know on whose account this calamity has come upon us.' So they cast lots, and the lot fell on Jonah. He said to them, 'Pick me up and throw me into the sea; then the sea will quieten down for you; for I know it is because of me that this great storm has come upon you.' So they picked Jonah up and threw him into the sea; and the sea ceased from its raging. But the Lord provided a large fish to swallow up Jonah; and Jonah was in the belly of the fish for three days and three nights.

Everyone knows the story of Jonah and the Whale – except that there is no whale but a 'large fish'. But for most people perhaps the story ends with Jonah being cast up safely on dry land. In fact the main point comes after this, when he succeeds in calling the people of Nineveh to repent and then sulks because God has spared them. He has to learn that God's love is for all and his pardon is unconditional for those who turn to him. It is worth reading this whole short book through. It is probably an old folk tale which a later writer has taken and developed to show that the God of Israel was also the God of the whole world. Jonah tries to avoid an unwelcome duty to which God calls him, sails in an opposite direction and settles down to sleep while others are in danger. After a terrifying experience, he finds himself where he should have gone directly. He is selfish to the end, but God can still use him in his service. But how much easier it would have been for everyone if he had been obedient from the beginning.

Think of something that you know is your Christian duty but do not want to do. (This exercise of imagination will probably be an easy one!) It may be quite a simple thing: to visit someone in need whom you find boring, to write a helpful letter or to be more disciplined in devotion. You have promised to follow Christ on your journey through life, but when the going becomes difficult you fall back and block your own hope of progress. Think of other people in sorrow, trouble, loneliness, while you sleep or follow an easy way of pleasure. Then, like the shock of plunging into cold water, feel the call that rouses you from your selfishness and do what you should have done before.

How often do I refuse to do what I know is right? Do I think that sin is only doing wrong or do I feel the equal seriousness of failing to do good?

Thank God for the shocks and surprises of life that recall us to the right way. Praise the loving purpose that is stronger than our selfish resistance.

⬥

I am convinced that Jonah knew better than anyone the purpose of his message to the Ninevites, and that, in planning his flight, although he changed his place, he did not escape from God. Nor is this possible for anyone else, either by concealing himself in the bosom of the earth, or by soaring on wings, if there be any means of doing so, or by any other of the many devices for ensuring escape. For God alone of all things cannot be escaped from or contended with, if he wills to seize or bring them under his hand.

St Gregory Nazianzen

*

Almighty Father, calling sinners to repentance and using even the weak and selfish to bring the good news, forgive my love of ease, my unwillingness to serve, and make me an instrument of peace even when my will rebels.

Lord, keep me always in the right way.

Week 2: Thursday

Journey Day by Day
Matthew 2, part of verses 1–12

In the time of King Herod, after Jesus was born in Bethlehem of Judea, wise men from the east came to Jerusalem, asking, 'Where is the child who has been born king of the Jews? For we have observed his star at its rising, and have come to do him homage.' When King Herod heard this, he was frightened, and all Jerusalem with him; and calling together all the chief priests and scribes of the people, he inquired of them where the Messiah was to be born. They told him, 'In Bethlehem of Judea.' Then he sent them to Bethlehem saying, 'Go and search diligently for the child; and when you have found him, bring me word so that I may also go and pay him homage.' When they had heard the king, they set out; and there, ahead of them, went the star that they had seen at its rising, until it stopped over the place where the child was. On entering the house, they saw the child with Mary his mother; and they knelt down and paid him homage. Then, opening their treasure-chests, they offered him gifts of gold, frankincense and myrrh.

❖

'A cold coming we had of it,' T. S. Eliot wrote of the journey of the Magi, echoing a sermon by the seventeenth-century divine Lancelot Andrewes. These 'Wise Men' would be followers of a cult which practised magic and divination and gave great attention to signs in the stars. They were not kings, as later legends suggested, but probably men of little wealth, travelling simply and able to meet little more than their basic needs. (It is worth reading the whole of Eliot's poem 'Journey of the Magi' for an imaginative account of the discomforts of their journey.) They travelled on, day by day, without full understanding of their purpose, knowing only that they were being led by a star of unusual significance. They may have wondered why they, Gentiles from another land, were called to worship the King of the Jews. When they came to the man who claimed that title, they knew that this was not the end of their quest and went on until they found a newborn baby. They knelt and worshipped him, giving him presents traditionally representing his kingship, priesthood and sacrificial death. We know this passage as the Gospel for Epiphany, the end of the twelve days of Christmas. But we hear only the end of their story and perhaps do not reflect on the long journey which they had taken in faith: a faith as yet imperfect but used by God to bring them into his incarnate presence and to be a sign that salvation was for the Gentiles as well as the Jews.

Imagine yourself on a long journey, far from home and uncertain of your destination. Every night you have to seek for shelter in a strange place, among people of a different language and culture. It is cold at night, and sometimes a place to rest is hard to find, and sleep imperfect when it is found. After a few hours you must start again on the weary way, knowing only that there is a sign that must be followed to the journey's end.

Do I demand certainty and clear knowledge of what God is calling me to do? Is his call to the Christian life enough to keep me journeying towards him, without continually reaching after certainty?

Thank God for the faith that is sufficient for each day. Praise him for the guidance of holy scripture and the gift of prayer.

❖

Christ himself is this star; it is he that enlightens and purifies the heart, teaching it to look up and by his own sweet attractive influence within, leading us on to himself, to the manifestation of himself in great love and lowliness.

Isaac Williams

*

Alone with none but thee, my God,
I journey on my way.
What need I fear when thou art near,
O King of night and day?
More safe I am within thy hand
Than if a host did round me stand.
                              St Columba

Christ, be my guiding star today.

Week 2: Friday

Journey in Fear
Matthew 2:13–15

An angel of the Lord appeared to Joseph in a dream and said, 'Get up, take the child and his mother and flee to Egypt, and remain there until I tell you; for Herod is about to search for the child, to destroy him.' Then Joseph got up, took the child and his mother by night, and went to Egypt, and remained there until the death of Herod.

◈

This was a strange journey, an episode that is not generally included in our Christmas readings, though it is the prelude to the Massacre of the Innocents remembered on 28 December. The Magi travelled with hardship, but in hope of an end that would crown their journey. The Holy Family went away by night, driven by the warning of danger to the life of the beloved baby of whom so much had been promised. The command to go into Egypt would make the journey seem even more threatening. It was the land of former slavery, the land from which Israel had been delivered and brought to freedom. It seemed as if all were being reversed, as if God's promises were being revoked and the one who had been declared as the Saviour had to go back into the place of captivity. But the great purpose of God would again be revealed: this was a symbolic repeating of the first deliverance, leading to a greater one. For Jesus, it was the first of many journeys and wanderings that would follow in the years of his ministry, until the last and most terrible journey to Jerusalem and the Cross.

Think of how the fear of that first night of escape has been felt by millions of people in the years that have followed. Can you begin to imagine the sufferings of refugees, driven from their homes by war, persecution, famine? Picture the travellers with no destination, with no incentive except the drive to move on. Let your heart go out to them: it is too much to grasp with real understanding but try to open yourself to the love and pity of God for all who suffer. As you seek spiritual progress this Lent, be sure that your devotions do not become selfish. Let them strengthen your compassion and intercessions. When you seem to be drawn away from the safe, familiar ways, when it seems as if what has been built up is being torn apart, pray that your trust in God will be strengthened. Every journey has a beginning and an ending, and if the beginning is in doubt and fear, the end will be in a new revelation of God's purpose.

Do I continue to trust God when I am afraid, when a problem seems too great, a situation too threatening? Do I remember to pray for the refugees and homeless, and do I give what material help I can?

Thank God for all the guidance you have received and not recognized at the time. Praise him for the joys that have begun in anxiety.

⬦

S uffer me not to judge according to the sight of the outward eyes, nor to give sentence according to the ears of ignorant men; but to discern with true discrimination between things seen and things spiritual, and above all things ever to seek thy good will and pleasure.

Thomas à Kempis

*

G racious Lord, keep me strong in faith and hope when I am in doubt, as firmly as when life is following my own desire. Bless me when I am anxious and uncertain about the future and keep me in the right way. Have mercy on all who wander with no resting-place, and all whose minds are restless because they do not know the love that is in Christ.

There is no fear when God is leading.

Week 2: Saturday

Journey for the Gospel
Acts 14:1, 2, 5–7, 19–20

In Iconium Paul and Barnabas went into the Jewish synagogue and spoke in such a manner that a great many of both Jews and Greeks became believers. But the unbelieving Jews stirred up the Gentiles and poisoned their minds against the brothers. And when an attempt was made by both Gentiles and Jews, with their rulers, to maltreat them and to stone them, the apostles learned of it and fled to Lystra and Derbe, cities of Lycaonia, and to the surrounding country; and there they continued proclaiming the good news. But Jews came there from Antioch and Iconium, and won over the crowds. Then they stoned Paul and dragged him out of the city, supposing that he was dead. But when the disciples surrounded him, he got up and went into the city. The next day he went on with Barnabas to Derbe.

◇

John Wesley wrote in his Journal on 29 August 1762, 'While I was preaching, several things were thrown, and much pains taken to overthrow the table; and after I concluded, many endeavoured to throw me down.' Others, before and after him, have shared the experience of St Paul in being persecuted for preaching the gospel. They were all following the command of Jesus at the time of his Ascension, to bring the message of salvation to the whole world. St Paul was the first to teach the full meaning of the New Covenant that was for all people everywhere who would receive it. He made many journeys, suffered much and eventually died as a martyr. So the Church has grown through the work of missionaries and teachers, often in danger and privation. God's messengers have made their journeys into the unknown, some to distant lands and some to the unconverted close to them. These have been journeys taken in faith, without looking for reward. If you read the whole of this chapter of Acts, you see how the people of Lystra at first worshipped Paul and Barnabas as gods and then turned against them. On our journey through life, when we meet disappointments and feel let down, let us remember that we are sharing the experience of the Apostles and of our Lord himself.

Think of yourself setting out on a journey to a place where the people have never even heard of Jesus Christ. They may be indifferent, mocking, hostile or violent to the point of killing. What would you say to them? Would your actions show the love that was in your words? You are quite alone, without the support of family, friends or church. Only God is with you and you are sent to do his work. Think of these things and then con-

sider the opportunities that are close to you, the
people you may be able to bring to Christ by showing his love for them in their situations. Your
missionary journey may not be so demanding as
those that St Paul took, but there is still work to
be done.

Do I confirm my faith by my way of life? Do I
show the love of God in my relationships? Do I
depend too much on the approval of others and
fear to speak of my faith?

Thank God for all the people who have led you to
faith and helped you on your spiritual journey.
Praise him for the freedom that the gospel brings.
Pray for missionaries and evangelists.

> Teach me, dear Lord, to serve thee as thou
>   deservest:
> To fight and not to heed the wounds,
> To toil and not to look for rest,
> To labour and not to seek for any reward
> Save that of knowing that I do thy will.
>   *Ignatius Loyola*

*

As I travel through this season, grant me the faith that has given strength to those who have gone before me on the journey, and grace to follow their good example in showing that faith through word and deed until the journey ends.

Lord, take my lips and speak through them.

Week 3: Mountains

Not many of us have attempted the great feats of mountaineering which attract public attention, but we all know what it is like to climb even quite a small hill and stand on its summit. There is a new sight of the surrounding countryside, laid out and extending far beyond what we can see when we stand at its own level. There is a new vision: details which previously seemed to be separate are now seen as part of a wider pattern. Although we do not think that heaven is 'up there', somewhere in the sky, we do feel lifted up from the earth, closer to God in the stillness. It is on the mountain top that God often reveals himself to people in the Bible. As we meditate on some of these mountain experiences, we can relate them to our own lives. These are moments on the journey when we take time to go apart, to renew our commitment and to assess our spiritual state more deeply than in our regular daily devotions.

Week 3: Monday

Mountain of the Law
Exodus 24:12, 15–18

The Lord said to Moses, 'Come up to me on the mountain, and wait there; and I will give you the tablets of stone, with the law and the commandments, which I have written for their instruction.' Then Moses went up on the mountain, and the cloud covered the mountain. The glory of the Lord settled on Mount Sinai, and the cloud covered it for six days; on the seventh day he called to Moses out of the cloud. Now the appearance of the glory of the Lord was like a devouring fire on the top of the mountain in the sight of the people of Israel. Moses entered the cloud, and went up on the mountain. Moses was on the mountain forty days and forty nights.

Mount Sinai was the mountain of the Law, where Moses was entrusted with the commandments on which the religion of Israel was to rest. The Law of God is for ever and cannot be changed by human preference or destroyed by our rejection. By grace given in Christ, we are forgiven when we go against God, are sorry and want to be reconciled for a fresh start. We have been freed from the fear of judgement that will accept no defence and the despair of knowing that we continually fail even when we want to be obedient. Let us never use our freedom in Christ as an excuse for indifference. 'As servants of God, live as free people, yet do not use your freedom as a pretext for evil' (1 Peter 2:16). The idea of an easy-going God who simply indulges whatever we choose to be and to do has no place in the Bible. Today as much as ever the world needs stability and assured values. Too many people think that what seems right for the individual needs no further justification. The life that follows selfish desires and does not seek to know the will of God in all things is not the Christian life.

Have you been in a lonely place and felt the wonder and majesty of God? To come even a little way from the bustle of our crowded lives is a renewal of the peace that he gives when we truly desire it. Think of the immense distances, the utter isolation, of the desert above which Moses climbed to hear the divine will. Stand on Mount Sinai and think of that awesome presence. God comes to Moses in all his majesty, like a devouring fire which tests but does not destroy. He comes to us in every moment of our lives, testing us with the fiery tongues of the Holy Spirit, strengthening us by the silent power of the Spirit within us. Whenever you pray, begin by knowing that you are in the presence of God and adoring him for his perfect Being.

Which commandments do I most often break? Ask for strength to be more obedient to the eternal Law.

Do I properly acknowledge the love of God which does not condemn the repentant sinner? Give thanks for the Power that is more ready to forgive than to condemn.

⬥

Take away, O Lord, the veil of my heart when I read the scriptures. Blessed art thou, O Lord: O teach me thy statutes! Give me a word, O Word of the Father: touch my heart, enlighten the understandings of my heart, open my lips and fill them with thy praise.

Lancelot Andrewes

*

Almighty God, I praise the gracious love that meets us in the deep valley as well as on the high mountain. Grant that I may both rejoice in the marvellous freedom brought by Jesus Christ, and be obedient to the commandments that he fulfilled and did not destroy.

Love God and keep his commandments.

Week 3: Tuesday

Mountain of Resignation
Deuteronomy 34:1, 4–6

Moses went up from the plains of Moab to Mount Nebo, to the top of Pisgah, which is opposite Jericho, and the Lord showed him the whole land. The Lord said to him, 'This is the land which I swore to Abraham, to Isaac, and to Jacob, saying, "I will give it to your descendants"; I have let you see it with your eyes, but you shall not cross over there.' Then Moses, the servant of the Lord, died there in the land of Moab, at the Lord's command. He was buried in a valley in the land of Moab, opposite Bethpeor, but no one knows his burial place to this day.

❖

This is the end of the forty years of wandering in the wilderness, when the Israelites come to the border of the Promised Land. Moses climbs a mountain as he had done to receive the Law on Mount Sinai. (The names Pisgah and Nebo come from two traditions of Bible record.) The choice of Pisgah probably reflects its mention as the place from which Balaam saw and blessed the Israelites on their journey (Numbers 23:14–26). Moses has led them out of Egypt, taught them, rebuked and encouraged them, and shared in their privations. In the chapters before this passage, he has given them further instruction about the next stage in their life, blessed them in their tribes and appointed Joshua as his successor. Yet he can only look upon the Promised Land and will not enter it. Some have thought that it was because of his own failures or because of the collective sins of his people. Perhaps we need only see it as the end of an era; it is time to let go and hand the future to a younger person. We all need to let go when God requires it, and not only in old age. There are many times in our lives when we must let someone else continue what we have begun. Moses was granted a sight of the land which the Lord had prepared. He died confident of a great future for his people.

You are climbing a mountain. It is steep, the day is hot and the ground is hard, but you hope that if you can cross this mountain you will find great happiness. You reach the top and look down on the most beautiful land that you have ever seen. You long to make the descent and come closer to that vision. But you are held back: this is enough and the distant vision is all that you can have. You throw yourself on the ground, despondent, resentful that all your exertion has brought so little. Then you realize that the sight of beauty is a gift from God, who will grant or withhold according to his purpose. You kneel, thank him for his mercies, rejoice with those who are living in the beautiful valley and prepare to return, strengthened in faith by the splendid vision.

Do I expect always to be thanked and rewarded for what I do? Do I resent it when others get credit for my work? Am I really pleased when I hear of people enjoying what I have not got?

Thank God for all the sights of beauty. Thank him for the opportunities of working for his sake alone.

❖

We must wait for God, long, meekly, in the wind and wet, in the thunder and lightning, in the cold and the dark. Wait, and he will come. He never comes to those who do not wait.

Frederick Faber

Lord, if it be for thy honour, let this be done in thy name. Lord, if thou dost see that this is expedient, and dost approve it as profitable for me, then grant that I may use it to thy honour. But if thou knowest that it will be hurtful to me, and not profitable for the salvation of my soul, take away from me such a desire.

Thomas à Kempis

*

*A**lmighty God, guide and protector of all who follow in faith, grant me the perfect love that rejoices with those who rejoice and does not turn away for any disappointed hope. Open my eyes to see the creating love that has made all, and the caring love that sustains all.*

We are all children of the Promise.

Week 3: Wednesday

Mountain of Temptation
Matthew 4:8–11

The devil took Jesus to a very high mountain and showed him all the kingdoms of the world and their splendour; and he said to him, 'All these I will give you, if you will fall down and worship me.' Jesus said to him, 'Away with you, Satan! for it is written, "Worship the Lord your God, and serve only him."' Then the devil left him, and suddenly angels came and waited on him.

❖

John Milton's great epic poem *Paradise Lost* tells of the Fall of the human race. When he wrote a sequel as *Paradise Regained*, his theme was the story of the temptation of Jesus in the wilderness. The final victory over sin and death was won on the Cross, towards which our devotions are directed in Lent, but it is good to remember the importance of those forty days in which our Lord confronted evil and overcame its false offers. Here was the beginning of a restoration to that original righteousness of which we have already thought: perfect humanity bridged the gulf between fallen humanity and God. The first temptation of Jesus, to assuage his hunger by turning stones into bread, was dismissed as readily as he always refused to use his divine power for his own advantage. But here was something different: the establishment of the reign of the Son of God without the Cross, without long years of waiting for all to be gathered in, without the sufferings that would come upon generations of Christians. But the price was the ultimate sin, of calling evil good, of making a deliberate choice to use its power rather than patiently obeying the will of God. It seemed a little thing, a moment of obeisance that would soon be over. Jesus proclaimed the supremacy of God, and turned to the way that would lead to Calvary.

You are still on the mountain from which you looked into the beautiful valley. You have thanked God for the sight of it and are preparing to descend the way you came. But a new thought comes to you. If you go down on the other side, surely there is so much that you can do for God. Your old life seems to be making no progress; you have done what you can, and it is time to move on. Just going down the mountain a different way would be only a little disobedient. You cannot stay where you are, and it would be a waste of that strenuous climb just to look and return. God cannot really have meant you to go back, if you want to do his work as well as finding new pleasures for yourself. Then above the valley you see a great cross, the price that Jesus paid for absolute obedience to the will of his Father.

How often do I tell myself that a wrong action is justified because it may lead to good? A little lie makes the situation more comfortable or some of the money not really due to me can be given to charity. Do I invent specious moral reasons to justify what I want to do?

Thank God for the conscience that makes us able to distinguish between right and wrong, and the grace that gives us strength against temptation. Praise him for the example of Jesus, who in his humanity knew temptation but not sin.

❖

> O wisest love, that flesh and blood,
>   Which did in Adam fail,
> Should strive afresh against the foe,
>   Should strive and should prevail.
>   *J. H. Newman*

*

Almighty God, in whose Son Jesus Christ we have both a pattern of obedience and a power that saves us from the power of sin, grant that I shall resist all that would turn me away from the path of salvation, and follow him through all the temptations of this life.

Worship the Lord your God, and serve only him.

Week 3: Thursday

Mountain of Teaching
Matthew 5:1–11

When Jesus saw the crowds, he went up the mountain; and after he sat down, his disciples came to him. Then he began to speak, and taught them, saying,

> *'Blessed are the poor in spirit, for theirs is the kingdom of heaven.*
> *Blessed are those that mourn, for they will be comforted.*
> *Blessed are the meek, for they will inherit the earth.*
> *Blessed are those who hunger and thirst for righteousness, for they will be filled.*
> *Blessed are the pure in heart, for they will see God.*
> *Blessed are the peacemakers, for they will be called children of God.*
> *Blessed are those who are persecuted for righteousness, for theirs is the kingdom of heaven.*
> *Blessed are you when people revile you and persecute you and utter all kinds of evil against you falsely on my account.'*

◈

The 'Sermon on the Mount' – of which this is only part of the first section – has attracted many people who may know little more about the Christian faith. Perhaps they have a picture of Jesus going to a high place from which he could address a great crowd of people – and this is what illustrations to this passage sometimes show. He gives them simple instructions about how they should live: here is plain ethical teaching without any need for 'religion'. The reality is quite different. As the previous verses tell us, Jesus had attracted a vast number of people by his miracles of healing. He goes up the mountain to get away from the crowd and gathers his disciples around him. These may not have been only the Twelve, but they were his close followers. What they hear is far from simple morality. It is a reversal of worldly values, promises of blessing for those whom the world might regard as inadequate or unfortunate. There is no promise of an easy life; those who follow him may find their way leads to contempt and even persecution.

You are there, close to Jesus. Perhaps you have become one of his followers. Or perhaps you have come from curiosity about this new teacher who has performed such wonderful cures, have climbed the mountain with the others and slipped in quietly among them. What are you expecting to hear? How to cure sick people? How to keep the Law and interpret it in your daily life? How to gain some secret knowledge such as you have heard that the mystery religions of the time possess? Read the words of the passage again, trying to meet them as if for the first time. How do they relate to you? Do you want to accept these blessings with all that they mean for living? There is much more of this 'sermon'; find time to read further and reflect upon what you read.

Do I really try to follow the teaching of Jesus, not for merit or reward but simply from love, and gratitude for the way of salvation? Am I ready to accept the new responses that are continually asked of me?

Thank God for the guidance of the Bible. Praise him for the love that allows us knowledge of his will in language that we can understand.

❖

The one Master alone fit to teach matters of so great importance, teaches on a mountain. There he teaches sitting, as behooves the dignity of the instructor's office; and his disciples come to him, in order that they might be nearer in body for hearing his words, as they also approached in spirit to fulfil his precepts.

St Augustine

*F*ather in heaven, who has given us the scriptures, and especially the gospel of our Saviour,
to guide us through this world, give us also a deep
love of these holy words, and a true desire to live
in the way of his commands.

**Blessed are they who hear the word of God and
obey it.**

Week 3: Friday

Mountain of Glory
Mark 9:2–8

Jesus took with him Peter and James and John, and led them up a high mountain apart, by themselves. And he was transfigured before them, and his clothes became dazzling white, such as no one on earth could bleach them. And there appeared to them Elijah with Moses, who were talking with Jesus. Then Peter said to Jesus, 'Rabbi, it is good for us to be here; let us make three dwellings, one for you, one for Moses, and one for Elijah.' He did not know what to say, for they were terrified. Then a cloud overshadowed them, and from the cloud there came a voice, 'This is my Son, the beloved, listen to him!' Suddenly when they looked around, they saw no one with them any more, but only Jesus.

❖

Again Jesus goes up into a mountain. He has shown the perfection of his humanity on the mountain of temptation, and his authority as a teacher on the mountain where he gathered his disciples around him. Now he goes with only three of his closest friends, the 'inner circle' of the Twelve, to a mountain traditionally identified as Mount Tabor but perhaps Mount Hermon. Now it is the full glory of his divinity that is revealed. The appearance of Moses and Elijah, men who had experienced the presence of God on mountains, signifies the Law and Prophets of the Old Covenant, now fulfilled and drawn into the New Covenant through the incarnate Son of God. The three disciples see the glory of God, the *Shekinah* which was revealed to a favoured few in the old Israel. The cloud from which the divine voice is heard often appears in these revelations, as the cloud covered Mount Sinai when Moses received the tablets of the Law. Note the reaction of Peter, always the first to speak and often getting it wrong. He wants to stay on the mountain but the vision fades and they descend. The following verses tell how Jesus immediately responds to a call for healing and resumes his ministry.

Think of the most wonderful things in your life, a time when you have felt the near presence of God and the assurance of his love. It may be in private prayer or public worship, perhaps in experience of beauty in nature, music or painting, or perhaps through a much loved person. You are on the heights, lifted above ordinary living, and you long to stay there for ever. Surely this is what God desires for you? But again you must go back. There is work to do, more of life's journey to be followed. God is as near to you in the valley as on the summit. The glory that he has shown you is still around you, even though you may not see it. You cannot be always on the mountain but you can draw strength from its vision.

Am I always open to God's revelations to me? Do I use the times of special grace to influence my daily life? Do I sometimes resent the routine calls of duty and regard myself as specially privileged above others?

Thank God for the many ways in which he reveals himself. Praise and adore the supreme revelation in Jesus Christ, divine glory in human life.

❧

Thou wast transfigured on the mountain, and thy disciples beheld thy glory, O Christ our God, as far as they were able to do so: that when they saw thee crucified, they might know that thy suffering was voluntary, and might proclaim unto the world that thou art truly the brightness of the Father.

Orthodox Liturgy

*

Almighty God, maker and sustainer of all creation, open my eyes to see the signs of glory: in worship, in all kinds of beauty, in other people, and grant me the patient love that finds glory in daily tasks and simple service.

We have beheld his glory.

Week 3: Saturday

Mountain of Agony
Luke 22:39–46

Jesus came out and went, as was his custom, to the Mount of Olives, and the disciples followed him. When he reached the place, he said to them, 'Pray that you may not come into the time of trial.' Then he withdrew from them about a stone's throw, knelt down, and prayed, 'Father, if you are willing, remove this cup from me, yet not my will but yours be done.' Then an angel from heaven appeared to him and gave him strength. In his anguish he prayed more earnestly, and his sweat became like great drops of blood falling down on the ground. When he got up from prayer, he came to the disciples and found them sleeping because of grief, and said to them, 'Why are you sleeping? Get up and pray that you may not come to the time of trial.'

The Mount of Olives stands to the east of Jerusalem. Here Jesus often went with his disciples, and from it he had ridden into Jerusalem on the humble back of a donkey. Now he goes to Gethsemane, an olive-grove on its lower slope.

After the times of temptation, of teaching and of glory he has come to Jerusalem, weeping over it for its rejection of the divine revelation and foretelling its destruction. A few days before he had been hailed by an excited crowd. Now he has only his closest followers with him. One has gone to betray him and the others have fallen asleep while he wrestles with the knowledge of what the following day must bring. Temptation returns, the natural human wish to avoid suffering and escape death. But he has always used his power for others, never for himself. As in the wilderness, human flesh and blood again triumph over the call of evil and offer perfect obedience to the divine will. We dare not try to fathom the mystery further.

It is dark, the time of night when resistance is at its lowest. You are awake while all the rest of the world seems to be sleeping. Think of the night terrors, those hours when all seems lost and trouble overwhelms you. There is no comfort; even those dearest to you are asleep and unknowing. That is only a tiny fraction of the suffering of our Lord in Gethsemane. Nothing exists now but you, and God who has made you and brought you to this moment. You call on him, remember his promises and wait until he brings you from darkness into light.

Can I watch with my Lord without becoming weary? Do I fulfil the times set apart for prayer, or do I fall away into other things? When I say the Lord's Prayer, do I sincerely say, 'Thy will be done'?

Thank God for the assurance of his love in the darkest times, the grace that keeps the Christian soul from the sin of despair. Praise the name of the Saviour who knows, with more than divine omniscience, the experience of human terror.

⬥

The Lord, when he had wished to demonstrate to us, even in his own flesh, the flesh's infirmity, by the reality of suffering, said, 'Father remove this thy cup'; and remembering himself added, 'save that not my will, but thine, be done'. Himself was the Will and the Power of the Father: and yet, for the demonstration of the patience which was due, he gave himself up to his Father's Will.

Tertullian

*

Good Lord, give me grace, in all my fear and agony, to have recourse to that great fear and wonderful agony that thou, my sweet Saviour, hadst at the Mount of Olivet before thy most bitter passion, and in the meditation thereof, conceive spiritual comfort and consolation profitable for my soul. St Thomas More

Not as I will, but as God wills.

Week 4: Light

Light is perhaps the most powerful, the most basic and the most widely shared image of God. From pagan worship of the sun to the spiritual significance of light in the Gospels, people have recognized the mystery of light and its negative side of darkness. As we take our journey and climb our mountains, we need the light of God to keep us in the right way. This week we shall think of some of the many ways in which the Bible interprets the meaning of light, and we pray that our lives shall be lived in the wonderful light that God gives us.

Week 4: Monday

Light of Creation
Genesis 1:1–5

In the beginning when God created the heavens and the earth, the earth was a formless void and darkness covered the face of the deep, while a wind from God swept over the face of the waters. And God said, 'Let there be light'; and there was light. And God saw that the light was good; and God separated the light from the darkness. God called the light Day, and the darkness he called Night. And there was evening and there was morning, the first day.

❖

The Bible begins with a declaration of light as the first and basic act of creation. We can only speak in these terms of time, since the ultimate mystery of timelessness is beyond our grasp in this life. Light is the image of there being anything instead of nothing, of the difference between being and non-being. All that follows in creation rests upon the division between light and darkness. This is a truth that the writers of the Bible continually remember and express in various ways. The Psalms give us words to declare, 'The Lord is my light and my salvation' and to acknowledge our dependence on God, 'In thy light shall we see light' (Psalms 27:1; 26:9). In a passage often read as part of the preparation for Christmas, the Prophet writes of the mercy of God towards Israel, 'The people that walked in darkness have seen a great light: they that dwell in the land of the shadow of death, upon them hath the light shined' (Isaiah 9:2). The light of God's glory breaks upon the shepherds who first hear of the birth of Jesus (Luke 2:8–9), and St John tells of the coming of Christ, 'The true light' (John 1:9). In relating the separation of day and night, the writer of Genesis reminds us of the rhythm which gives a firm framework to our lives, and later tells of God's promise to Noah that the rhythm will be maintained and that the seasons, and day and night, will not cease (Genesis 8:22). Light continually reveals the glory of creation: but it also shows us the harm that we have done to it and reminds us that we are not masters but stewards of what God has made.

You are in total darkness. Perhaps it is a sudden power cut or a moonless night in a lonely place. You have no sense of direction, no knowledge of what is around you. Even what is familiar by day or in accustomed artificial light is no longer under your control. You begin to doubt the reality of the world which a little time ago was unquestioned as the background of your normal experience. Even your own reality seems to be slipping away. Suddenly light returns to the room or you reach a well-lit road. Confidence surges back and you move freely, soon forgetting the short time of deprivation. You feel more thankful for blessings which you have been taking too much for granted. But you also become more aware of the disorder of your life. The light which gives power to move freely is also a call to start tidying up and doing a bit of cleaning.

Do I let God's light shine freely in my life so that I can honestly confront my sins? How often do I prefer not to face reality?

Thank God for the gift of light, for the light of the eye and the light of the soul. Praise him for the love that has given order and pattern to human life.

If ye hearken to the Light in you, it will not suffer you to conform to the evil ways, customs, fashions, delights and vanities of the world; and so lead you to purity, to holiness, to uprightness, even up to the Lord.

George Fox

*

*E*ternal Light, shine into our hearts,
*Eternal Goodness, deliver us from evil,
Eternal Power, be our support,
Eternal Wisdom, scatter the darkness of our
    ignorance,*

Eternal Pity, have mercy upon us,
  that with all our heart and mind and soul
  and strength we may seek thy face and be
  brought by thine infinite mercy to thy holy
  presence.

Alcuin of York

The Lord is my light and my salvation.

Week 4: Tuesday

Light of Guiding
Exodus 13:18, 21; 14:9, 19–22

God led the people by the roundabout way of the wilderness towards the Red Sea. The Lord went in front of them in a pillar of cloud by day, to lead them along the way, and in a pillar of fire by night, to give them light, so that they might travel by day and by night. The Egyptians pursued them, all Pharaoh's horses and chariots, his chariot drivers and his army. The angel of God who was going before the Israelite army moved and went behind them; and the pillar of cloud moved from in front of them and took its place behind them. It came between the army of Egypt and the army of Israel. And so the cloud was there with the darkness, and it lit up the night; one did not come near the other all night.

◈

A much-loved hymn is 'Guide me, O thou great Redeemer' – or 'great Jehovah' in some versions – by the Welsh writer William Williams. It has the lines 'Let the fire and cloudy pillar/Lead me all my journey through', inspired by this passage which tells of how God led the Israelites out of Egypt and showed them the right way to follow through unknown territory. The sun gives light to the whole world, and the light of God fills our lives if we will open ourselves to let it shine on us. Sometimes, however, we need a special light to show the way through a dark place, and there are times when a new situation or a difficult decision brings us to ask for special grace and guidance. The Bible continually tells of how individual men and women have been shown the next step in their lives, and often turned back from a way that would have led to disaster. Sometimes it was a clear light like the pillar of fire which left no doubt of where to follow. Sometimes it was more like the cloud, leading on step by step but with no long vision of the meaning. We have all known both of God's ways of leading us on, and like the Israelites we have tried to follow in faith. When we reject divine guidance and insist on going our own way, life is darkened and our self-will becomes a cloud between us and God. By his grace, we find the way back, but continual obstinate rejection can make us enemies of God who prefer darkness to light because their deeds are evil (John 3:19).

You are walking across a big open place in the dark, holding a little pocket torch which lights only a very short way in front of you. Suddenly you come within range of a sensor which switches on a powerful light to illuminate the whole area. You see that you have strayed a little from the direct path and now the way forward is clear. But it looks quite a long way compared with the shortcut that could be made from where you have reached, and you set off again in the direction of your choice. After a time the light goes out and you are left with your own tiny light, uncertain how to continue and not knowing what obstacles may be in your way. Your only hope is that you will somehow get back into range of the sensor again. We are proud of our little torches. Some are called 'intellect', others 'wealth', others 'rank' or 'authority'; and there is a very popular model which some call 'good deeds' and others 'decent living'. They all look pale and insignificant when we step into the light of God's providence.

Do I like to go my own way without considering if it is the way that in my heart I know is God's way for me? Do I trust in my own strength to stop me from going astray?

Thank God for guidance all through your life, to this day, and to this time of Lenten devotion. Praise him for the loving care that does not leave us to travel alone.

◈

L ead, kindly Light, amid the encircling
    gloom,
    Lead thou me on;
The night is dark, and I am far from home,
    Lead thou me on.
Keep thou my feet, I do not ask to see
The distant scene; one step enough for me.

                                        J. H. Newman

*

B e thou my vision, O Lord of my heart,
Be all else as naught to me, save that
thou art,
Be thou my best thought by the day and the
night,
Both waking and sleeping, thy presence my
light.

                              Old Irish, trans. Mary Byrne

The Word of God is my guiding light.

Week 4: Wednesday

Light of the World
John 1:1-9

In the beginning was the Word, and the Word was with God, and the Word was God. He was in the beginning with God. All things came into being through him, and without him not one thing came into being. What has come into being with him was life, and the life was the light of all people. The light shines in the darkness, and the darkness did not overcome it. There was a man sent from God, whose name was John. He came as a witness to testify to the light, so that all might believe through him. He himself was not the light, but he came to testify to the light. The true light, which enlightens everyone, was coming into the world.

❖

The Prologue to the Fourth Gospel takes us deep into the Christian revelation, in words that speak to our hearts rather than our intellectual understanding. We know this passage as the Christmas Gospel, unfolding the mystery of the Incarnation in our joyful celebration of the Nativity. Let us now remember that Christ came to suffer and die for us: the Child of Bethlehem grows into the Man on the Cross. He not only gives light to the world but is himself that light. Creation and guidance are wonderful, but the living presence of God among us is more wonderful still. He says, 'I am the light of the world' (John 8:12). You have probably seen the famous picture by Holman Hunt with that title. Jesus stands at a door overgrown with briars – the sins which turn us away from him. He carriers a lantern and knocks on the door: the painter combines the theme of light with another saying, 'Behold, I stand at the door and knock' (Revelation 3:20). Not everyone today likes the style of this Victorian painting, but it conveys a message that is worth attention. We must put away our sins and let the light come in.

You are comfortable in your private room with the door closed, settled in your favourite chair with enough light for what you are doing – perhaps relaxing over a book, listening to music or pursuing some other pleasant occupation. It has been a long and busy day and you feel entitled to a little time to yourself. Then there is knocking on the door, gentle but urgent at the same time. Is it someone you want to see, perhaps bringing you some new pleasure or benefit? Or is it someone with a need that will take up your time of leisure? Eventually you get up and open the door a little way, and a great light begins to enter. It is immeasurably bright but not dazzling, and as you open the door further it floods into the room and all that was comfortably familiar now seems shabby and insignificant. Sit and be quiet in the wonder of Christ the Light.

Do I let my selfish concerns shut out the divine light? Am I living in the full power of life that God offers me?

Thank God for every sign and token of his presence. Praise him for the coming of Christ, the Light of the World.

❦

O thou, who art the light of the minds that know thee, the life of the souls that love thee, and the strength of the wills that serve thee: help us so to know thee that we may truly love thee, so to love thee that we may fully serve thee, whom to serve is perfect freedom.

St Augustine

*

*C*hrist, whose glory fills the skies,
    Christ the true, the only light,
Sun of Righteousness, arise
    Triumph o'er the shades of night;
Dayspring from on high, be near;
Daystar, in my heart appear.

Charles Wesley

Christ be my light today and every day.

Week 4: Thursday

Light of Choosing
John 3:16–21

*God so loved the world that he gave his only
Son, so that everyone who believes in him may
not perish but may have eternal life. Indeed,
God did not send the Son into the world to
condemn the world, but in order that the world
might be saved through him. Those who believe
in him are not condemned, but those who do
not believe are condemned already, because they
have not believed in the name of the only Son
of God. And this is the judgement, that the light
has come into the world, and people loved darkness rather than light because their deeds were
evil. For all who do evil hate the light and do
not come to the light, so that their deeds may
not be exposed. But those who do what is true
come to the light, so that it may be clearly seen
that their deeds have been done in God.*

Years ago I overheard a conversation in a
French restaurant. A diner asked what on the
menu was particularly good, to which the waiter
replied, 'Tout est bon, vous n'avez que choisir'
– 'Everything is good, you only have to choose.'

Unfortunately, life is not usually so simple and not everything that we can choose is good. The human tendency to take the wrong way is expressed in the story of the Garden of Eden and appears many times in the Bible in the stark alternatives of choosing blessing or cursing, light or darkness, life or death. God has a purpose for each of us and will guide us if we will follow, but he has also given us freedom of choice, freedom to go wrong if we take that way. This passage comes after the meeting of Jesus with Nicodemus, who is told that he must be born again and become a new man to enter the Kingdom of God. To be born again is to turn to Jesus, who is blessing, light, life. The salvation which he offers is absolute and overcomes all our sins, but we need to respond. The light which guides us also reveals us as we are. If one continually chooses the darkness, there is the terrible possibility of finally rejecting God, of saying in the words that Milton gives to Satan:

So farewell hope, and with hope farewell fear,
Farewell remorse; all good to me is lost;
Evil be thou my good.

Think of a divided path which offers two ways that you can take. One is wide and smooth, but so dark that you can see only a little way ahead. The other is brightly lit but it leads steeply upwards and is stony under foot. You take what looks like the easier way, but it soon proves to be full of obstacles and strange shapes which are frightening in the darkness, so you turn back and thankfully follow the way of light. Think of a time in your life when you went astray, perhaps from misjudgement or perhaps because the decision was clearly wrong but attractive. How did God call you back, make you bless the way that is difficult but does not fear the fullness of his light? Has he brought light into your darkness this Lent?

Do I take responsibly my power to choose my way? Do I always ask for God's guidance when I am in doubt? How often am I afraid to step into his clear light?

Give thanks for the light of Christ that shines through our doubts and perplexities. Praise the divine love that sent the Son to be the Saviour of the world.

❖

May the Lord Jesus put his hands on our eyes also, for then we shall begin to look not at what is seen but at what is not seen. May he open the eyes that are concerned not with the present but with what is yet to come, may he unseal the heart's vision, that we may gaze at God in the Spirit, through the same Lord Jesus Christ, whose glory and power will endure throughout the unending succession of ages.

Origen

*

*A*lmighty God, who set my way before me and gave me grace to follow not in fear but in love, grant that I shall always turn away from darkness into the light that leads to salvation.

Love the truth and follow the light.

Week 4: Friday

Light of Change
Acts 26:9, 12–18

I was convinced that I ought to do many things against the name of Jesus of Nazareth. With this in mind I was travelling to Damascus with the authority and commission of the chief priests, when at midday along the road I saw a light from heaven, brighter than the sun, shining around me and my companions. When we had all fallen to the ground, I heard a voice saying to me in the Hebrew language, 'Saul, Saul, why are you persecuting me? It hurts you to kick against the goads.' I asked, 'Who are you, Lord?' The Lord answered, 'I am Jesus whom you are persecuting. But get up and stand on your feet, for I have appeared to you for this purpose, to appoint you to serve and testify to the things in which you have seen me and to those in which I will appear to you. I will rescue you from your people and from the Gentiles – to whom I am sending you to open their eyes so that they may turn from darkness to light and from the power of Satan to God, so that they may receive forgiveness of sins and a place among those who are sanctified by faith in me.'

This is St Paul's own testimony to his conversion. The phrase 'Damascus Road' is often used to describe an experience which changes a person's belief and attitude, not always in matters of religious faith. Many have known a similar moment of conviction which has started them on the Christian way. For others, probably for the majority of believers, faith has grown from early years and become a regular part of life. Yet to be a Christian is always to know the powerful light of Christ that guides and teaches us. Saul is thrown to the ground by its force, temporarily blinded until he receives new sight to obey what God has called him to do, and sees the whole world in a different way. This is the call of the gospel: to be born again as Nicodemus is told, to leave the old ways and follow the new. Saul the persecutor of the Church was changed on the Damascus Road into its most fervent missionary, even changing his name, or perhaps adopting a second name which he already had. He continually exhorts his converts to be true to the revelation that they too have known. The light of Christ can destroy in order to create, taking away so that more can be given. We who keep this Lent may think that as Christians we need no Damascus Road; but being a Christian is to be always open to new calling and fresh insight.

You are back in the dark room where the light has failed. It is a rather shabby and untidy room, positively dirty in places, but it is comfortable and you do not want to make the effort of any changes. The light suddenly comes on again. The room is still there, still recognizable and yet different. It is cleaner, some things have been replaced, others moved around. You are surprised, uncomfortable, resentful at this interference with what has long been familiar. Yet at the same time you feel strangely excited about the new possibilities. You open the door, and again all outside is the same and yet different. It needs resolve to walk out into that clear light, but you feel sure that all is well.

Am I always open to receive new calls from God? Do I realize that my sin is a constant hurt to him?

Thank God for the shocks and surprises that have changed your life for the better. Praise him for all who have helped you to know him more clearly.

❖

This man who is so frantic as even to shed blood and cast men into prisons, all at once believes! It was not enough that he had never been in Christ's company: the believers must be warred upon by him with vehement hostility. But when he was blinded, then he saw the proofs of his sovereignty and divine kindness: then he answers, 'Lord, what wilt thou have me to do?'
                                        St John Chrysostom

Dear Lord, wounded by my sins, resisted by my stubborn and selfish will, bring me back into the right path when I wander away and open my eyes to see the light of truth.

In thy light we shall see light.

Week 4: Saturday

Eternal Light
Revelation 21:22–4; 22:3–5

I saw no temple in the city, for its temple is the Lord God the Almighty and the Lamb. And the city has no need of sun or moon to shine on it, for the glory of God is its light, and its lamp is the Lamb. The nations will walk by its light, and the kings of the earth will bring their glory into it. The throne of God and of the Lamb will be in it, and his servants will worship him; they will see his face, and his name will be on their foreheads. And there will be no more night; they need no light of lamp or sun, for the Lord God will be their light, and they will reign for ever and ever.

<hr />

The Bible begins and ends with light. At the moment of creation God says, 'Let there be light.' Now, in the vision of heaven which the author of the Book of Revelation tries to express in human language, the marvel of divine light is taken up again and made perfect. The sun and moon were created so that we might have light and know the rhythms of night and day. In the presence of God they are no longer needed, for he is absolute light as he is absolute goodness, mercy and love. In a sense we limit his infinity by naming any of his attributes, but we have no other way of trying to come close to him while we are in this world. We cannot decipher the ultimate mystery, but the words of those who have been granted special insight can give us all we need. Now in the middle of Lent, we do not cease to adore God for his glory. Thanksgiving, penitence, petition and intercession are all essential aspects of prayer, but prayer should always begin with adoration, praising God not for what he does in us but for his very Being.

Sit quietly and let the light of God enfold you. Feel the radiance of his love pouring out through the angels, the saints of all ages, the work of the Church. Feel it in the love of those who love you and have helped to bring you to this time of adoration. Draw it into the depth of your being. Send it out again in love to them, to all who are keeping this holy season in penitence and faith, to the whole world. Do not try to remember all the needs of individuals and nations, for they are too much for our minds to grasp. Let everything be drawn into the radiance of God, the eternal light. Be still, and let God love you as you are.

And as we come to the end of our week of meditating on the light of God, let us find its completion in the words of scripture:

It is he alone who has immortality and dwells in unapproachable light, whom no one has ever seen or can see; to him be honour and dominion.

1 Timothy 6:16

We cannot see him with mortal eyes, but by his grace we shall one day see him as he is.

Do I face my sins honestly, remembering that one day I must see them in the light of God himself? Do I always praise and adore God in my prayers, or do I only ask for things I want?

Thank God for the promise of eternal life through Jesus Christ. Praise him for the glory that we cannot comprehend but know that we may hope to share after death.

◦◈◦

Your enjoyment of the world is never right, till every morning you awake in heaven. See yourself in your Father's palace; and look upon the skies, the earth, and the air as celestial joys: having such a reverent esteem of all, as if you were among the angels.

Thomas Traherne

*

Do thou, Christ, deign to kindle our lamps, our Saviour most sweet to us, that they may shine continually in thy temple, and receive perpetual light from thee, the light perpetual, so that our darkness may be driven from us.

St Columbanus

Eternal light, shine on me.

Week 5: Food and Drink

We do not need to be reminded that food and drink are essential for our lives. We soon become aware of hunger if we have to wait for a longer time than usual without eating. We know also the pleasure of meals, not least as a way of sharing fellowship. All these aspects appear in the Bible: God gives our daily food and has pity on the hungry, his people know the pleasures of a feast, and they are happy together as they eat. We thank him for the good things of this world, but we also see them as signs of spiritual grace. Jesus tells his followers to hunger and thirst for righteousness. In stories of eating and drinking, we find ways in which we grow nearer to him.

In this week, let us make a special offering of some abstinence in food or drink, as thanksgiving for our own sustenance, and to strengthen our intercession for the millions in the world who are continually hungry.

Week 5: Monday

Water of Strife
Exodus 17:1, 3–7

*The whole congregation of the Israelites jour-
neyed by stages as the Lord commanded. They
camped at Rephidim, but there was no water
for the people to drink. But the people thirsted
for water; and the people complained against
Moses and said, 'Why did you bring us out of
Egypt, to kill us and our children and our live-
stock with thirst?' So Moses cried out to the
Lord, 'What shall I do with this people? They
are almost ready to stone me.' The Lord said to
Moses, 'Go on ahead of the people, and take
some of the elders of Israel with you; take in
your hand the staff with which you struck the
Nile, and go. I will be standing there in front
of you on the rock at Horeb. Strike the rock,
and water will come out of it, so that the people
may drink.' Moses did so, in the sight of the
elders of Israel. He called the place Massah and
Meribah, because the Israelites quarrelled and
tested the Lord, saying, 'Is the Lord among us
or not?'*

The going was hard. The Israelites had escaped from slavery in Egypt, been brought miraculously across the sea and guided on their way by the divine presence in cloud and fire. But soon the desert showed its menace in the lack of water. Parched and weary, they forgot all that Moses had endured and done for them, forgot even God's merciful protection and broke into angry recriminations. Why had they listened to the promise of redemption? Even the life of a slave was preferable to death by thirst. Once more, in his infinite love and patience, God had mercy on them and provided for their physical need. The memory of their sin of ingratitude remained for centuries in the conscience of the nation. They did not forget the day of provocation and temptation in the wilderness when they had striven against God and put him to the test (Psalm 95:8). The miracle of water was remembered as 'the water of strife' (Psalm 106:32). It was a type of the disobedience for which the Prophets continually called them to repentance.

Try to imagine terrible thirst. You have probably never felt its extremity, though millions in the world know it daily. You can think of nothing except water. How soon the body takes over and dominates our higher nature. You rage in your misery; perhaps you blame God and accuse him. He who suffered in human flesh understands, pities and pardons. But how vividly you remember the benison of cool drink, wish you had valued it more fully and long for even a little now. Think how little gratitude you felt for such mercies, how little you valued them. Then you reach a spring of fresh water and soon your thirst is relieved. All is well again and you resume your life, resolved never again to take God's gifts for granted.

Do I blame God when things go wrong? Do I sometimes resent the demands of Christian faith upon my life and wish that I was not so committed to God's commandments? Do I always thank him when life is good?

Thank God for all that keeps your body in health and strength. Praise him for his unending patience with you and with all who too easily turn away from him in difficulties.

❖

O ur trust is often not complete, because we are not sure that God hears us, as we think, because of our unworthiness and because we are feeling nothing at all; for often we are as barren and dry after our prayers as we were before. And thus when we feel so, it is our folly which is the cause of our weakness, for I have experienced this in myself. And our Lord brought all this suddenly to my mind and said: I am the ground of your beseeching.

Julian of Norwich

*

God our Father, who brought water out of the rock so that the people should not perish, give me a thankful heart for the gifts that sustain me in this world and a deep thirst for the loving obedience that honours the Giver.

God gives us the water of life freely.

Week 5: Tuesday

Food for Service
1 Kings 19:1, 3–8

Ahab told Jezebel all that Elijah had done, and how he had killed all the prophets with the sword. Then he [Elijah] was afraid; he got up and fled for his life. He went a day's journey into the wilderness, and came and sat down under a solitary broom tree. He asked that he might die. 'It is enough, now, O Lord, take away my life, for I am no better than my ancestors.' Then he lay down under the broom tree and fell asleep. Suddenly an angel touched him and said to him, 'Get up and eat.' He looked, and there at his head was a cake baked on hot stones, and a jar of water. He ate and drank, and lay down again. The angel of the Lord came a second time, touched him, and said, 'Get up and eat, otherwise the journey will be too much for you.' He got up and ate and drank; then he went in the strength of that food for forty days and forty nights to Horeb the mount of God.

❖

Elijah had had enough. He had fearlessly done the Lord's work, culminating in a spectacular contest with the priests of Baal which had proved the supremacy of the God of Israel. Jezebel, the pagan wife of weak King Ahab, had a longstanding feud with him and was after his blood. He was ready to give up, weary of his task, weary of life itself. The divine calling to be a prophet had brought him nothing but toil, and eventually danger to his life. When Elijah was at the lowest ebb, God met him in both his physical and his spiritual need – how often these are connected in the stories of the Bible. Food and drink revive the body and also show God's loving care. Elijah received strength for the next stage in his calling, the journey to the sacred Mount Horeb, where God had given water from the rock. There he met the very Spirit of God in a 'still, small voice'. Then, filled with new spiritual power, he brought Ahab to repentance after yet another grave sin, and prepared Elisha to be his successor as a prophet. The whole story is a lesson to persevere in obedience. As G. K. Chesterton said, the point about Christianity is not that it has been tried and found wanting, but that it has been found difficult and not tried.

Remember some great disappointment you have suffered: work done with no result and no credit, a strong hope frustrated, lack of support by those from whom you expected help. Yes, remember it now in all its bitterness: do not conceal the hurt from yourself. As a Christian you will have done your best at the time to take it well, not to brood upon it and feel resentment. That was good: but was some of the hurt driven inside, suppressed but not really cleansed? Resentment is one of the most destructive emotions eating away at the good in us, and it can be worse when we pretend to ourselves that it has gone. Set the memory free to be itself, and also remember the many times that good has come out of apparent failure. What valuable lessons have you learned, and how often have you taken a different way forward, helped by a strength that was not your own? Now really kill that resentment which you were half enjoying. Eat and drink the spiritual food that God provides.

Do I give up easily when the Christian way becomes hard? Is this Lent seeming tedious and discouraging? Or do I think that I should have more credit and reward for my acts of obedience?

Thank God for all the times he has brought you out of despair into new hope. Praise him for all that he provides to keep us going in body and soul.

❖

Thou that givest food to all flesh, who feedest the young ravens that cry unto thee and hast nourished us from our youth up: fill our hearts with good and gladness and establish our hearts with thy grace.

Lancelot Andrewes

God will keep you firm to the end.

Week 5: Wednesday

Food of Growth
Psalm 23

The Lord is my shepherd, I shall not want.
He makes me lie down in green pastures:
he leads me beside still waters;
he restores my soul.
He leads me in right paths
for his name's sake.
Even though I walk through the valley of the
shadow of death,
I fear no evil;
For you are with me;
your rod and your staff – they comfort me.
You prepare a table before me
in the presence of my enemies;
you anoint my head with oil;
my cup overflows.
Surely goodness and mercy shall follow me
all the days of my life,
and I shall dwell in the house of the Lord
my whole life long.

❖

This is the best known and loved of all the
Psalms. It has been many times rendered into
verse and sung as a hymn. Generations of Chris-

tians have found special comfort in its image of God's loving care. But it is more complex than it may appear. It begins with the familiar idea of God as a shepherd, a thought which was very dear to a pastoral community depending a great deal on its flocks. Isaiah says that God 'will lead his flock like a shepherd' (40:11) and Jesus speaks of himself as the Good Shepherd (John 10:11–18). In this Psalm we first hear how God will give his people the food and drink they need, the green pastures and the still waters. He will protect them with the rod or club that drives away wild beasts and the staff that guides the flock in the right way. Even as they go through a dark valley – or as we often hear it 'the valley of the shadow of death' – they are not afraid because he is with them. Then there is a new thought. The Psalmist is no longer like a sheep but like an honoured guest at a banquet, justified against accusers, fed not with grass and water but with choice food and wine, anointed like a priest or a king. Yesterday we thought how we must persevere in the Christian life: here is a promise not only of continuity but of growth. We are to mature, be ready to grow in grace, while we still acknowledge our dependence.

You have been trying to follow a Christian way of life, trusting in God and fulfilling the duties which accompany faith. Perhaps it has become a routine: the private prayer, the churchgoing, the acts of kindness and charity. They are sincere enough, but are they still exciting and challenging, or are they repetitions of a pattern over many years? But suddenly something more is required of you. Your faith is tested by a more difficult task or the opening of a new and more advanced way of devotion. Then the past must seem a silent preparation for a step forward to higher things. Your work for God may be known only to you and to him, but it is a call you cannot refuse. You come from the peaceful but familiar green fields where sheep are grazing into a brightly lit room filled with splendour. You stand amazed at first and then receive these new gifts in the love of God. Be ambitious as well as humble. Jesus tells us to be as little children and St Paul says that we must in time put away childish things. The words they use are different in Greek: in English, quite simply, we are to be *childlike* but not *childish* in our faith.

Has my Christian life become just a routine? Am I really trying to make progress this Lent? Am I growing up in faith?

Thank God for his leading and protection to this moment. Ask for the nurture that makes us even closer to him.

To despond because we are what we are, what is this but still, in a subtle way, to imply that it is in our own power to become otherwise? So only would it follow that if our affections are not at once changed, as we would, this is our present sin and that we have not a heart right with God at all. But this is to suppose that we ourselves can make or mould or remake our own hearts.

E. B. Pusey

*

*L*oving Shepherd, guide and protector, lead me in the way appointed for me, giving me wisdom to discern the richer food of holiness and grace to receive it for the strengthening of my soul.

Goodness and mercy will follow me all my life.

Week 5: Thursday

Hunger of Obedience
Matthew 4:1-4

Then Jesus was led up by the Spirit into the wilderness to be tempted by the devil. He fasted for forty days and forty nights, and afterwards he was famished. The tempter came and said to him, 'If you are the Son of God, command these stones to become loaves of bread.' But he answered, 'It is written, "One does not live by bread alone, but by every word that comes from the mouth of God."'

◆

A man who had been a prisoner in the Far East during the war once told me that, among all the privations and sufferings, the thought of food was dominant for much of the time. Few of us have experienced extreme hunger, though millions in the world are habitually without enough to eat, but we know how even a temporary lack of food can affect our concentration and our temper. Jesus had fasted for forty days – the length of Lent in which we try to come closer to his example. How easily he, the Son of God by whom all things were made, could have satisfied his raging hunger. Our Lord never performed a miracle for his own comfort or advantage: he had set aside his divine power to become fully human, and he refused no discomfort or pain of our mortal condition. He dismisses the temptation with a scriptural reminder that our souls need the word of God as much as our bodies need food (Deuteronomy 8:3).

You have thought about extreme thirst. Now try to imagine hunger greater than anything you have known. Forty days and nights have passed through burning heat by day and intense cold at night in this desert place where you have gone to pray and to meditate on what you are called to do in this world. Could you still value the things of the spirit before the things of the flesh? Think of those who have suffered extreme hunger and other privation, and yet have kept the faith and brought it to others. Ask for greater strength to resist the temptation of compromising faith and integrity for present satisfaction.

Am I keeping my little rule of fasting or abstinence? Am I keeping it with weary resignation, with self-satisfaction, or as a true act of free obedience?

Thank God for the grace that allows the will to keep faith when the feelings are rebellious. Pray for those who have too little to eat, and for those who are enslaved by bodily desires.

Jesus was fasting in the desert. All the needs of life were at rest. In a momentary freedom from this slavery, earth had no hold on him. None can tell to how great a degree of liberty, independence, and spiritual freedom, a soul absorbed by God may bring its own body. Time exists no longer for the spirit which God withdraws from all terrestrial things, from all which can change and perish, and steeps in his eternal light.

Henri Lacordaire

The chief mystery of our holy faith is the humiliation of the Son of God to temptation and suffering.

J. H. Newman

O God, who by our great Master's example, hast taught us what labours and sufferings heaven deserves, and that we are to take it by force, confound in us, we beseech thee, the nice tenderness of our nature, which is averse to the discipline and hardship we ought to endure as disciples and soldiers of Jesus Christ; help us on our way thither, by self-denial and mortification.

John Wesley

*

B *lessed Lord, who suffered the pains of hunger without yielding to temptation, give me wisdom to recognize the first attack of temptation and grace to stand firm in the truth which is the bread of life.*

I am hungry for the Word of God.

Week 5: Friday

Food of Compassion
Mark 6:34–6, 38, 41–4

Jesus saw a great crowd; and he had compassion for them, because they were like sheep without a shepherd; and he began to teach them many things. When it grew late, his disciples came to him and said, 'This is a deserted place, and the hour is now very late; send them away so that they may go into the surrounding country and villages and buy something for themselves to eat.' He said to them, 'How many loaves have you? Go and see.' When they had found out, they said, 'Five, and two fish.' Taking the five loaves and the two fish, he looked up to heaven, and blessed and broke the loaves, and gave them to his disciples to set before the people; and he divided the two fish among them all. And all ate and were filled; and they took up twelve baskets full of the broken pieces and of the fish. Those who had eaten the loaves numbered five thousand men.

❖

This remarkable story is the only one of the miracles of Jesus that is described in all four Gospels, with only slight differences of detail. It is a strange story but the witness for it is strong and it was clearly an event which the early Christians regarded as important. For those who follow it in faith, it has several things to teach. The miracle is performed as an act of compassion for hungry people in a difficult situation. Not only did Jesus never use his divine power for his own benefit: he never used it simply as a spectacle to demonstrate that power. His miracles were acts of love, not of magic. Then we read how the meal was not only sufficient for urgent need. There was more than the hungry crowd could manage, as there had been a great provision of wine at the Cana marriage (John 2:1–12). God's bounty is not like our measured giving. Further, the action of Jesus prefigures what he did at the Last Supper: he took bread, gave thanks, broke it and gave it. This is what is done at every Christian Eucharist, and the Gospel writers record it as a sign of the even greater miracle that was to come.

It has been an exciting day. You have been one of the crowd who followed this new teacher and healer of whom you have heard so much. The power of his words and the company of others filled with the same enthusiasm have made you forget about eating and about the distance you have walked. Now it is late, the day is colder and you are a long way from either home or the chance of buying food. The excitement fades; your spirits are low and your body cries out for food. Perhaps you even begin to grumble about religious people who are full of pious words but do nothing to help physical needs. Then those who are close to the leader start organizing everyone into groups. This seems just another delay before you can eat, but you sit down for want of anything better to do. Then you find yourself eating, offered more than you can possibly take. And with the food comes a new contentment, a sense of fellowship with strangers who have shared your need and now share your satisfaction. Eventually the crowd disperses. Do you walk away, glad to be no longer hungry, or do you want to stay with the one who has shown you such love?

Am I grateful for the food I eat? Do I accept physical wellbeing as a right? Do I share the compassion of Jesus for the needs of others?

Thank God for all that enables you to live well and comfortably in this world. Praise the divine love that cares for all our needs.

❖

*L**ord** whose love never fails and whose compassion meets us in our weakness and need, as my body is fed from the bounty of creation, so may my soul be fed by grace, to be in fellowship with all the faithful who are the Body of Christ, now and for eternity.*

Bread of Heaven, feed me now and evermore.

Week 5: Saturday

Food of Salvation
1 Corinthians 11:23–7

I received from the Lord what I also handed on to you, that the Lord Jesus on the night when he was betrayed took a loaf of bread, and when he had given thanks, he broke it and said, 'This is my body that is for you. Do this in remembrance of me.' In the same way he took the cup also, after supper, saying, 'This cup is the new covenant in my blood. Do this, as often as you drink it, in remembrance of me.' For as often as you eat this bread and drink this cup, you proclaim the Lord's death until he comes. Whoever, therefore, eats the bread or drinks the cup of the Lord in an unworthy manner will be answerable for the body and blood of the Lord.

❖

St Paul's words follow the Gospel story of the Last Supper and link it specifically with the Christian Eucharist. We recall the fourfold actions of Jesus in the feeding miracle that we considered yesterday, now performed to even more wonderful purpose on the last night of his earthly life. It is the night of betrayal, the eve of his Passion. We feel particularly close to this moment when we hear the words of institution during Lent, the time when the Cross is most strongly in our minds. Before giving himself in the flesh for the salvation of the world, Jesus empowers his followers for the sacrament that will make him ever present with them. We have thought much about the divine giving of food for both body and spirit, but there has never been any so wonderful as this. Christians have faithfully followed our Lord's command and example. There are differences about exactly what is being done, but no question about why we are doing it: 'Do this, in remembrance of me.' But let us not forget St Paul's warning not to take the sacrament lightly. We can never be fully worthy of so great a gift, but we must offer our unworthiness in penitence and faith.

One of life's great pleasures is a meal among friends, and especially with someone deeply loved and trusted. You are enjoying just such an occasion, but this time there is a feeling of disquiet; all is not well. The loved one has talked about going away and of betrayal from within the group. The fellowship which has been so strong and beautiful is breaking up and the future is uncertain. Then the one whom you fear that you are about to lose does something which reminds you of another time together, when you were able to help in the work of compassion. This time it is different, more solemn and yet more joyful in spite of forebodings. You end the meal and go out together into the darkness. We cannot hope, cannot dare, to try to share the exact feelings of the disciples on that night. But our human experience may give us deeper reverence for the divine mystery. This is not a myth unfixed in time: it is the record of a night in history that is past, present and future.

Am I faithful and regular in receiving holy communion? Do I prepare myself for it and receive it reverently? Do I love and respect all my fellow-Christians with whom I cannot yet share this sacrament?

Thank God that you belong to the communion of believers, known and known, living, dead and yet unborn. Praise him for the Eucharist, which is itself the greatest Thanksgiving.

—◊—

Hunger and thirst, O Christ, for sight of thee
Came between me and all the feasts of earth.
Give thou thyself the Bread, thyself the Wine,
Thou, sole provision for the unknown way.
Long hunger wasted the world wanderer,
With sight of thee may he be satisfied.
                                        Radbod of Utrecht

Christ himself is our heavenly food.

Week 6: Healing

The quality of our lives depends a great deal on good health. Although many advances have been made in medical treatment, life today still brings problems of illness and injury. In the Bible, healing is seen as one of the gifts of God. The Gospels tell of many healing miracles done by Jesus, and these are often accompanied by words of pardon and salvation. One of the words much used in the Greek of the New Testament can refer equally to physical or spiritual healing. As we read some of the biblical healing stories, we may think of what we can learn from them about our own spiritual health and our response to God's saving power.

Week 6: Monday

Healing in Response to Prayer
2 Kings 20:1-5

In those days Hezekiah became sick and was at the point of death. The prophet Isaiah son of Amoz came to him, and said to him, 'Put your house in order, for you shall die; you shall not recover.' Then Hezekiah turned his face to the wall and prayed to the Lord, 'Remember now, O Lord, I implore you, how I have walked before you in faithfulness with a whole heart, and have done what is good in your sight.' Hezekiah wept bitterly. Before Isaiah had gone out of the middle court, the word of the Lord came to him: 'Turn back, and say to Hezekiah prince of the people, "Thus says the Lord, the God of your ancestor David, I have heard your prayer, I have seen your tears; indeed, I will heal you; on the third day you shall go up to the house of the Lord."'

Hezekiah was regarded as one of the best of the Kings of Judah. He was faithful to the pure worship of God, respected religious duties and sought for peace at a time when his people were threatened by foreign powers. He is stricken with an illness so severe that there seems to be no hope of recovery. He does not despair, or fall into anger and self-pity, but calls for help to the God in whom he trusted. His recital of his own virtues may not be commendable, but he makes an act of faith and is restored to the health which he seemed to have lost for ever.

Sickness of body or mind, together with other types of distress, must be faced as part of our human situation. At one time, and even today by some people, illness was regarded as a punishment for sin. Accepting the interaction of the physical and spiritual, and the fact that people may harm themselves by irresponsible behaviour, we should not blame the wrath of God when things go wrong. Sickness of any kind is not the desire of our loving Father. It is not a judgement on sin, but it may be seen as a result of the imperfection that human sin has brought into the perfect creation. We pray to him in his love, not as to a tyrant who needs to be appeased.

Think of bad times in your own life: perhaps actual illness, or depression, anxiety, broken relationship. How did you respond? Did you despair of things ever improving? Were you angry with God, thinking that you deserved better? Did you seek his guidance and help at once, or did you turn to him only when all efforts at self-help had failed? How would you respond now – has this Lent given you new insight?

Do I bring my griefs in prayer, or do I brood over them and think that nothing can be done? Do I really act as if I believe in the almighty power which I praise in hymns and public worship?

Thank God for all the times of healing in your life, physical, emotional or spiritual. Thank him for the power given to human agency in the work of healing and pray for those who tend the sick of mind or body.

It is God's will that we hold us in comfort with all our might: for bliss is lasting without end, and pain is passing and shall be brought to naught for them that shall be saved. And therefore it is not God's will that we follow the feelings of pain in sorrow and mourning for them, but that suddenly passing over, we hold us in endless liking.

Julian of Norwich

God often permits that we should suffer a little to purify our souls, and oblige us to continue with him. Take courage, offer him your pains incessantly, pray to him for strength to endure them. Above all, get a habit of entertaining yourself often with God, and forget him the least you can. Adore him in your infirmities, offer yourself to Him from time to time, beseech him humbly and affectionately (as a child his father) to make you conformable to his holy will.

Brother Lawrence

God of love, whose compassion never fails, we bring before thee the troubles and perils of people and nations, the sighing of prisoners and captives, the sorrows of the bereaved, the necessities of strangers, the helplessness of the weak, the despondency of the weary, the failing powers of the aged. O Lord, draw near to each, for the sake of Jesus Christ our Lord.

Anselm

*

Lord, keep me whole in body, mind and spirit, faithful when things are bad and thankful when they are good. Give me compassion for the suffering of others, and grace to do what work of healing I may.

God's power is made perfect in weakness.

Week 6: Tuesday

Healing of Scepticism
2 Kings 5:1, 9–14

Naaman, commander of the army of the king of Aram, though a mighty warrior, suffered from leprosy. He came with his horses and chariots, and halted at the entrance to Elisha's house. Elisha sent a messenger to him, saying, 'Go, wash in the Jordan seven times, and your flesh shall be restored and you shall be clean.' But Naaman became angry and went away, saying, 'I thought that for me he would surely come out and stand and call on the name of the Lord his God, and would wave his hand over the spot, and cure the leprosy! Are not Abana and Pharpar, the rivers of Damascus, better than all the waters of Israel?' But his servants approached and said to him, 'Father, if the prophet had commanded you to do something difficult, would you not have done it? How much more, when all he said to you was, "Wash and be clean"?' So he went down and immersed himself seven times in the Jordan, according to the word of the man of God; his flesh was restored like the flesh of a young boy, and he was clean.

How different from Hezekiah is the attitude of Naaman. He already feels defensive because of the horrible skin disease that has marred his otherwise successful career. When he comes to see Elisha he shows also a strong pride in the dignity of his position and a nationalistic contempt for the country he is visiting – human responses which are still only too common today. His servants, less demanding of special attention, persuade him to do what Elisha tells him, and the miracle of healing takes place. The story goes on to tell of his acceptance of the God of Israel, a request for some Israelitish soil on which he may worship at home, and a plea for pardon when he still has to go with the Syrian King into a pagan temple. He is a man who judges religion by its visible results; the simplicity of the command is justified in his eyes only when it has brought him some physical benefit.

Think of times when your dignity has felt affronted, when you have resented the lack of respect or special treatment that you thought due to you. Think of someone whose advice you have despised for its simplicity or because you regarded the giver as inferior to you in wisdom. Perhaps you have thought poorly of a person for being 'different' or 'foreign', of a country whose customs are different from your own. Think now of the simplicity of the faith and practice which is offered in Christ. There are no elaborate rituals of initiation, no degrees of knowledge to be attained, no secret mysteries to be mastered. God works through water, through bread and wine, through familiar language offered in prayer. His command is that we accept the love that is offered and to try to offer it back in our lives.

Do I patiently keep the simple rules of faith? Do I ever think that my intelligence, my position, my good works, make me a special sort of Christian?

Thank God for the way of faith that is open to all, without requiring special gifts. Praise him for the humility of the Incarnation.

———◇———

I come in the little things,
    Saith the Lord:
Not borne on morning wings
Of majesty, but I have set My Feet
Amidst the delicate and bladed wheat
That springs triumphant in the furrowed sod.
There do I dwell, in weakness and in power;
Not broken or divided, saith our God!
In your strait garden plot I come to flower:
About your porch My Vine
Meek, fruitful, doth entwine;
Waits, at the threshold, Love's appointed hour.
Evelyn Underhill

*

Gracious Lord, who took humble and obedient manhood for our sakes, open my eyes to see the simple signs of hope and to feel the gentle love that is around me through each ordinary day.

Have faith like little children.

Week 6: Wednesday

Healing and Pardon
Mark 2:3–12

Some people came, bringing to Jesus a paralysed man, carried by four of them. And when they could not bring him to Jesus because of the crowd, they removed the roof above him, and after having dug through it, they let down the mat on which the paralytic lay. When Jesus saw their faith, he said to the paralytic, 'Son, your sins are forgiven.' Now some of the scribes were sitting there, questioning in their hearts, 'Why does this fellow speak in this way? It is blasphemy! Who can forgive sins but God alone?' Jesus said to them, 'Why do you raise such questions in your hearts? Which is easier, to say to the paralytic, "Your sins are forgiven", or to say, "Stand up and take your mat and walk"? But so that you may know that the Son of Man has authority on earth to forgive sins' – he said to the paralytic – 'I say to you, stand up, take your mat and go to your home.' And he stood up, and immediately took the mat and went out before all of them; so that they were all amazed and glorified God, saying, 'We have never seen anything like this!'

❖

This is one of the most vivid and exciting stories about the healing work of Jesus in his years of ministry. His fame has already spread. He is surrounded by people wherever he goes, and so it will be for the rest of his life on earth. Except in the rare times when he can withdraw and be alone, or quietly with his closest followers, there will always be crowds – curious, demanding, praising for a few hours on Palm Sunday, hostile and murderous on Good Friday. It is the persistence of four friends that brings the sick man to him, a wonderful account of the power of human affection, and the determination to find healing against all difficulties. They make a hole in the roof: the Greek word *exorusso* is strong, ' to dig out', and archaeological excavations in Nazareth have found traces of houses with a layer of earth on a foundation of sticks above the main roofbeams. The healing is immediate and complete; the paralysed man walks away, carrying the bedroll on which he himself had been carried.

There is something more. Before the physical healing, Jesus pronounces forgiveness of sins. As we have seen, illness is by no means always the result of sin, and our Lord does not so regard it. But he wants people to be whole in every way, spiritually as well as physically healthy. His assertion of divine authority angers the religious teachers of the Law who are present. It is the first of the 'conflict stories' which will become more serious until the Passion.

Imagine being present on that day in Capernaum. Do you see yourself as sick and in need of healing? As one trying to help a sick friend? As a bystander who takes an objective view? As a Scribe who is shocked by the claim to forgive sin? Probably you understand all of these positions. You have known what it is to be dependent on others, in sickness or in some other difficulty. You have felt the love that wants to help the helpless. You have been aware of great faith events which have not deepened your own faith. You have been indignant when the familiar pattern of worship has been upset. Make a resolution to enter more fully into the Gospel stories and relate them to your own life.

Do I always give all the help I can to the sick and those in trouble? Do I make a real effort to be faithful in prayer and devotion when conditions are difficult?

Thank God for friendship and human compassion. Thank him for the love that restores us in body and soul.

❖

Hear further, O man, of the work of resurrection going on in yourself, even though you were unaware of it. For perhaps you have sometimes fallen sick, and lost flesh and strength and beauty; but when you received again from

God mercy and healing, you picked up again in flesh and appearance and recovered also your strength.

Theophilus of Antioch

*

Almighty God, grant me constancy in prayer and perseverance in the life of faith. Always, and especially at this season, may I so deeply regard the Passion of my Lord that my sins shall be forgiven and my infirmities healed, and I shall be made whole.

Jesus, pardon and restore me.

Week 6: Thursday

Healing through Faith
Luke 7:1–10

Jesus entered Capernaum. A centurion there had a slave whom he valued highly, and who was ill and close to death. When he heard about Jesus, he sent some Jewish elders to him, asking him to come and heal his slave. When they came to Jesus, they appealed to him earnestly, saying, 'He is worthy of having you do this for him, for he loves our people, and it is he who built our synagogue for us.' And Jesus went with them, but when he was not far from the house, the centurion sent friends to say to him, 'Lord, do not trouble yourself, for I am not worthy to have you come under my roof; therefore I did not presume to come to you. But only speak the word, and let my servant be healed. For I also am a man set under authority, with soldiers under me; and I say to one, "Go", and he goes, and to another, "Come", and he comes, and to my slave, "Do this", and the slave does it.' When Jesus heard this he was amazed at him, and turning to the crowd that followed him, he said, 'I tell you, not even in Israel have I found such faith.' When those who had been sent returned to the house, they found the slave in good health.

In Shakespeare's play *King Lear* the Earl of Kent, disguised and seeking fresh service with the master who has banished him, says to the King, 'You have that in your countenance which I would fain call master', and to the question, 'What's that?' replies simply, 'Authority.' The centurion had learned through long service to exercise and obey authority and in Jesus he recognized authority more powerful than military discipline. He knew that the simple word of command from him was enough to give healing, as surely as an officer's order would be passed on and put into effect. But he was too humble a man, despite his rank in the army of the occupying power, to expect a personal visit. He asked some of the Jews whom he had befriended to intercede with this new healer whose reputation had reached him.

Think of the centurion, a man accustomed to be instantly obeyed, as he waited to see if his humble request would be answered. We need no representatives to plead for us as the centurion sent influential Jews to make his request. Come to the Lord, oppressed by the anxieties and problems of the moment but trusting in his loving power. Today offer something that is troubling you, even if it seems small and trivial to other people, and ask him to take and heal it. Take another step forward towards stronger faith.

Do I at all times acknowledge the power of Jesus to heal and save? Do I recognize my unworthiness and trust in his redeeming love alone?

Thank God that the power which controls the universe works to heal the little things of this world. Thank him that as we come to him in prayer, he draws near to us and enters not only our homes but our inmost being. His great love does not balk at our unworthiness.

The man was his prayer, though he never formulated any prayer about it at all! And yet this man, mind you, this man was a Roman soldier, a heathen. He did not know the rules of the Sanctuary – not he! But the man knew his need, and his need drove him right up into the heart of his Maker.

Arthur Stanton

Gracious Lord, look mercifully on my unworthiness, and accept the faith that so often falters and hesitates but still trusts that I can be made clean. Let me trust in the assurance of the gospel that in the Cross there is pardon for all who truly seek it.

Lord, I am not worthy: but only say the word and I shall be healed.

Week 6: Friday

Healing of the Hopeless
Luke 8:43–8

There was a woman who had been suffering from haemorrhages for twelve years; and though she had spent all she had on physicians, no one could cure her. She came up behind him and touched the fringe of his clothes, and immediately her haemorrhage stopped. Then Jesus asked, 'Who touched me?' When all denied it, Peter said, 'Master, the crowds surround you, and press in on you.' But Jesus said, 'Someone has touched me; for I noticed that power had gone out from me.' When the woman saw that she could not remain hidden, she came trembling; and falling down before him, she declared in the presence of all the people why she had touched him, and how she had been immediately healed. He said to her, 'Daughter, your faith has made you well; go in peace.'

This is a strange episode, not only in its account of a miracle but also because of its position in the Gospel. Matthew, Mark and Luke all agree in placing it within the story of how Jesus restored to life the daughter of Jairus: as he is going to the house, the woman touches him. It is unusual for the narratives to be interrupted by a second narrative in this way, and the whole passage conveys a sense of something very striking which the witnesses remembered in detail. Again, a curious crowd is pressing around Jesus. Peter cannot believe that he would be aware of one touch in a jostling throng; some accounts add the comment of other disciples, in a tone almost of impatience. But Jesus can recognize the touch of faith and he grants immediate healing and a blessing of peace. Our Lord is the help of the helpless, the hope of those who have lost hope through long suffering, or despair after long continuance in sin. He cares for our smaller troubles as well as the great ones. Healing of a chronic complaint was less than restoring a child to a bereaved family, but an urgent need did not set aside his compassion for another sufferer.

Consider the burden of something very important to you, now or in the past. Perhaps it is a medical condition that was not responding to treatment; worry about work or money; difficulty in a relationship; sin lying heavy on the conscience. Put yourself in the Gospel story: feel the pressure of the crowd, the electric atmosphere of mingled hope, excitement and incredulity that surrounds this new Healer who is going to raise the dead. You are in the middle of it all, longing for his healing touch but feeling unworthy to approach him. Yet desperation forces you on, to touch his garment and fall at his feet. It was a painful struggle: but how easy it is to approach him in prayer and sacrament, to know his healing and peace. No trouble, no longing, is too small to bring to him. He who sustains all creation cares for the least of his creatures.

Do I always call on God for help, with the assurance of faith, in all my needs? Am I ever in danger of despair when sorrow or sin seem to hold me back? Am I allowing the failures in my rule this Lent to overshadow the spiritual graces God has given?

Thank God, who never turns away from those who seek him in faith. Adore the infinite love that responds to our weakness.

❖

Nothing in my hand I bring,
Simply to thy Cross I cling;
Naked, come to thee for dress;
Helpless, look to thee for grace;
Foul, I to the Fountain fly;
Wash me, Saviour, or I die.
                    Augustus Toplady

*

Almighty God, ever watching, ever caring, ever pardoning, make me clean both in body and soul. Strengthen my faith so that I may always walk in the way of peace.

Go in the peace of Christ.

Week 6: Saturday

Healing in the Name of Christ
Acts 3:1–8

One day Peter and John were going up to the temple at the hour of prayer, at three o'clock in the afternoon. And a man lame from birth was being carried in. People would lay him daily at the gate of the temple called the Beautiful Gate so that he could ask for alms from those entering the temple. When he saw Peter and John about to go into the temple, he asked them for alms. Peter looked intently at him, as did John, and said, 'Look at us.' And he fixed his attention on them, expecting to receive something from them. But Peter said, 'I have no silver or gold, but what I have I give you; in the name of Jesus Christ of Nazareth, stand up and walk.' And he took him by the right hand and raised him up; and immediately his feet and ankles were made strong. Jumping up, he stood and began to walk, and he entered the temple with them, leaping and praising God.

❖

The most striking impression on turning from the Gospels to *Acts* is the change in the Apostles. Even after the Resurrection they are still doubtful and frightened, unable to grasp what has happened. On the day of the Ascension they stand looking up into the sky until they are told to go and wait for the next command of God. After Pentecost, filled with the Holy Spirit, they are transformed. They preach, perform works of mercy and healing, begin to suffer persecution in the name of Jesus Christ. They speak confidently in the great city that is not their native place, and where their Master had been killed. The Jewish authorities take note that these simple and unlearned men 'had been with Jesus'. They show the power of the risen Lord, not a dead teacher but one in whom is the power of God, 'let loose into the world' as John Masefield says in his play *The Trial of Jesus*.

Imagine these things happening in your own town or village. A popular preacher, said to have per-formed some miraculous cures, has recently been condemned and executed for offences against the law. There has been a rumour that he has been seen alive. Now some men, not from your part of the country, are announcing this rumour as a fact and are doing in his name the kind of healing that he is said to have done. Reflect upon the strange-ness of it all. Would you have listened to the proc-lamation of good news? Think of the power that used very ordinary people to begin the Christian Church. Resolve that, as you hear and meditate again on the events of the Passion, you will not take them for granted as a familiar story but realize how wonderful they are.

Do I find many signs of God's power in my own life? Has my worship become too much a matter of routine?

Thank God for the strength which he gives to those who trust in him. Praise him for all those who still do his work of mission and mercy.

⬥

Of a truth it was marvellous. The Apostles did not urge him; but of his own accord he follows, by the act of following pointing out his benefactors. 'Leaping and praising God'; not admiring them, but God that wrought with them. The man was grateful.

St John Chrysostom

We are about to begin Holy Week, to remember the price of our redemption. In our worship we shall not be sad for wasted suffering but grateful for the sacrificial love that can change lives.

*

Be with me, Lord, as I prepare to keep this most solemn time, together with the whole Church. Open my eyes to see afresh the sorrows that have brought joyful redemption and grant me a deeper and stronger faith.

They had been with Jesus.

Holy Week

In this last week of Lent our devotions focus on the Passion of Christ. We shall think less of ourselves, less even of sorrow for our sins, and shall try to come closer to the Saviour whose suffering was the great price of our redemption. Each of the images of our lives which we have been considering in the past weeks has its place in the final story, and we use them to help us follow Christ and stand at the foot of his Cross. Some of the many reflections and prayers that have been inspired by the Passion may help our meditation.

Holy Week: Monday

Journey to Death
Luke 23:26-32

As they led him away, they seized a man, Simon of Cyrene, who was coming from the country, and they laid the cross on him, and made him carry it behind Jesus. A great number of the people followed him, and among them were women who were beating their breasts and wailing for him. But Jesus turned to them and said, 'Daughters of Jerusalem, do not weep for me, but weep for yourselves and for your children. For the days are surely coming when they will say, "Blessed are the barren, and the wombs that never bore, and the breasts that never suckled." Then they will begin to say to the mountains, "Fall on us"; and to the hills, "Cover us." For if they do this when the wood is green, what will happen when it is dry?' Two others also, who were criminals, were led away to be put to death with him.

❖

There had been many journeys taken at the command of God since Abram left Ur, and since the Children of Israel left Egypt. Jesus and his disciples had walked a long way during the years of his ministry. There had been rough roads, dark roads, lonely and weary days until a road led them from Galilee to Jerusalem for the week of the Passion. The last journey of all was short in human measurement, from the Roman headquarters to a hill on the outskirts of the city, but it was the most terrible and most wonderful journey that human feet have ever trodden. We cannot fully sense, even in loving imagination, the physical suffering of our Lord on the sorrowful way. The night of betrayal, desertion, denial, had ended in cruel mocking, scourging and sentence of death on the Lord of life.

Others were drawn into that suffering humanity. The drama of redemption needed its supporting cast to be complete. Simon of Cyrene, pressed into service by the hated occupying power, privileged to share the burden, traditionally converted to become one of the first Christian believers. Two violent criminals walking with Jesus: the sinless one numbered with sinners and suffering with them. The women who wept at the pitiful sight, drawing even from his bitter pain his compassion for the troubles that were to come upon Jerusalem in the next generation.

As I try this week to walk with my Lord,
May I remember Simon and be willing to
bear another's burden;
May I know myself to be a sinner, worthy of
the penalty which he took for me;
May I feel true sorrow for the suffering of
innocence, on that day and still today.
May I have grace to follow in the Way of the
Cross.

They laid the cross upon him as a malefactor.
He went forth bearing the cross as a trophy
over the tyranny of death: and as conquerors
do, so he bore upon his shoulders the symbol
of victory.

St John Chrysostom

Take up they cross, the Saviour said,
If thou wouldst my disciple be;
Deny thyself, the world forsake,
And humbly follow after me.

Charles Everest

Hold on, persevere, endure, bear delay and
thou hast borne the cross.

St Augustine

I saw the Son of God go by
Crowned with the Crown of Thorn.
'Was it not finished, Lord?' I said,
'And all the anguish borne?'

He turned on me His awful eyes:
    'Hast thou not understood?
Lo! Every soul is Calvary,
    And every sin a Rood.'
            Rachel Anand Taylor

*

Thanks be to thee, my Lord Jesus Christ,
  *For all the benefits which thou hast given
me,*
*For all the pains and insults which thou hast
  borne for me.*
O most merciful Redeemer, Friend and Brother,
May I know thee more clearly,
Love thee more dearly,
And follow thee more nearly.
          St Richard of Chichester

Take up thy cross and follow Christ.

Holy Week: Tuesday

Mountain of Suffering
Mark 15:22–7

They brought Jesus to the place called Golgotha (which means the place of a skull). And they offered him wine mixed with myrrh, but he did not take it. And they crucified him, and divided his clothes among them, casting lots to decide what each should take. It was nine o'clock in the morning when they crucified him. The inscription of the charge against him read, 'The King of the Jews.' And with him they crucified two bandits, one on his right and one on his left.

❖

Many of the mountain events in the Bible have brought people closer to God. Climbing above the level of daily life gives a stronger sense of his presence, and he reveals himself in the solitude of the heights. Now, in a place near Jerusalem, it seems as if God has withdrawn his protecting love. The sign of his glory is hidden in a dying man. On a mountain Jesus met and conquered temptation and showed how perfect humanity could resist evil. On a mountain he went apart to teach his disciples because his popularity had drawn crowds around him. On a mountain his divinity was revealed to a few chosen ones. Now it all seems to have been a failure. He who was declared Son of God in that moment of transfiguration is now naked, helpless, slowly dying.

It is not a very great mountain. It is a hill known as 'the place of a skull', perhaps because of its shape or perhaps because it was a common site for executions. The familiar name 'Calvary' is the Latin equivalent of the Hebrew name. The exact site has been disputed but legends grew up around it, particularly that it was the place where Adam was buried. The association has not a literal but a spiritual truth. Here the Second Adam brings to a terrible climax all the wrong that has come from human disobedience. The ultimate insult to God is made the way of salvation. St John reminds us that 'the place where he was crucified was near the city' (John 19:20). While that great love works to pardon us, people still pass by in ignorance and neglect, even in mockery of the Lord whom they will not recognize. The French writer Pascal wrote, 'Christ will be in agony until the end of the world.'

*

We can never match the love that is incomparable:
We do not know its fullness until we are made empty.
There is no place to stand now but the place of torment
where a naked hill beckons to the last encounter.

You who have had your seasons of conflict, will confess that it was not at Olivet that you ever found comfort, not on the hill of Sinai, nor on Tabor; but Gethsemane, Gabbatha, and Golgotha have been a means of comfort to you.

Charles Spurgeon

Inscribed upon the Cross we see
    In shining letters, 'God is Love';
He bears our sins upon the Tree;
    He brings us mercy from above.
Thomas Kelly

Am I a stone and not a sheep,
    That I can stand, O Christ, beneath
  thy cross,
To number drop by drop thy blood's slow
  loss,
And yet not weep?
Christina Rossetti

O my sweet Saviour Christ, which in thine undeserved love towards mankind so kindly wouldst suffer the painful death of the cross, suffer me not to be cold nor lukewarm in love again towards thee.

St Thomas More

*

*L*ord Jesus Christ, raised on a cross upon a hill, lift up my heart and soul above the waste places of my sin and accept my poor love that would respond to the immeasurable love given there.

I glory in the Cross of Christ alone.

Holy Week: Wednesday

Light Departed
Mark 15:33–4

When it was noon, darkness came over the whole land until three in the afternoon. At three o'clock Jesus cried out with a loud voice, 'Eloi, Eloi, lema sabachthani?' which means, 'My God, my God, why have you forsaken me?'

Darkness falls over the land, as the incarnate light of the world loses strength. The whole creation seems to be falling apart, returning to the primal chaos before God said, 'Let there be light'. It is the darkness that covered Egypt in the days of God's anger, the darkness in which the blind grope and wander, the darkness in which the betrayer goes out from the table of fellowship. Simeon saw in the infant Jesus the sign of a light to lighten the Gentiles. Now the ruthless power of a Gentile empire is putting out that light. Simeon prophesied also that a sword would pierce the soul of Mary. Now she stands by the Cross as her Child perishes and the humanity which began in her is leaving the world. The people that walked in light have seen a great darkness.

How can we respond to the horror of that noon of midnight? It is like the darkness of Hell, which Milton describes as 'Not light, but rather darkness visible'. We are helpless in the dark even though we can move and feel. Our Lord the uncreated, is now more helpless than any creature. Everything has gone from him: no friends but two or three who are faithful and desolate. He is deprived of clothes, of movement, fast losing the power of breath. What can we offer in the darkness but our doubts, our uncertainties, our weakness? There is no response but the love that feebly desires to respond to that breaking heart of divine love.

❖

After all their insulting, and their lawless derision, this is done, when they had let go their anger, when they had ceased mocking, when they were satiated with their jeerings, and had spoken all that they were minded; then He shows the darkness, in order that at least so (having vented their anger) they may profit by the miracle. For this was more marvellous than to come down from the cross, that being on the cross he should work these things.

St John Chrysostom

Lord Jesus Christ, Son of the living God, who for our redemption willedst to be born, and on the cross to suffer the most shameful of deaths, do thou by thy death and passion deliver us from all sins and penalties, and by thy holy cross bring us, miserable sinners, to that place where thou livest and reignest with the Father and the Holy Spirit, ever one God, world without end.

Pope Innocent III

Mary, Mother of Jesus, Mother of sorrow, pity the mothers who know their second agony,
the suffering and death of children,
the pain in the loins, the sword in the heart.

R.C.

O come all and let us sing unto him who was crucified for our sake; for seeing him upon the tree Mary spake: though thou sufferest crucifixion, yet art thou my son and my God.

Orthodox Kontakion

*

Lord, as we cry out of the darkness of sinful lives, hear and forgive.
Lord, as we cry out in tongues that cannot speak as they desire, hear and forgive.
Lord, as we cry out in the love that cannot match the divine love, hear and forgive.

Lord, lighten my darkness.

Holy Week: Thursday

Divine Thirst
John 19:28–9

After this, when Jesus knew that all was now finished, he said (in order to fulfil the scripture), 'I am thirsty.' A jar full of sour wine was standing there. So they put a sponge full of the wine on a branch of hyssop and held it to his mouth.

The Son of God has known human weariness, hunger, disappointment, pain. Now, as his human life ebbs, he feels the extremity of thirst. It has been many hours since he could drink, hours of mocking, scourging, the slow climb under the burden of the cross and above all the bleeding from brow and back, hands and feet. The divine power that gave water to a rebellious people in the wilderness does not intervene to bring a single drop of water. Only one of the guard, with a rough kindness, offers a sop of the sour wine that was the soldier's ration. The Evangelist reminds us of the words of the Psalmist, 'For my thirst they gave me vinegar to drink' (Psalm 69:21).

The physical suffering is extreme. But more is said and done here than the needs of the body.

The Bible often mentions thirst as an image of human desire for God.

> As a deer longs for flowing streams,
>   so my soul longs for you, O God.
> My soul thirsts for God,
>   for the living God. (Psalm 42:1–2)

Jesus has promised the living water, the water of life, to those who will love and follow him (John 4:10; 7:38). Does he now feel the withdrawal of God, as Matthew and Mark suggest in his cry from Psalm 22, 'My God, my God, why hast thou forsaken me'? Does he cry out not only in the flesh but in the desire to be again assured of divinity? Can God be forsaken of God? This is a terrible mystery in which we dare not seek further, but it seems as if the love of God penetrated even the human experience of spiritual desolation.

On this day, in our churches, we celebrate the institution of the Eucharist at the Last Supper. The wine that quenches thirst, the wine of human fellowship, becomes also the means of the divine presence. The wine that in the evening is declared to be the Blood of Christ now finds its fulfilment in the blood of his dying. His wounds complete the promise, assure us that the wine we offer will for ever be our communion with him.

❖

Run to the fountains for water, run swiftly, I say, be quick of foot like a hart. But who is this fountain? God, himself man. He it is that must and can cool the thirst of thy soul, he it is that will refresh thee.

St Augustine

I was moving about the world in search of the water of life. The things of this world – wealth, position, honour and luxury – looked like a lake by drinking of whose waters I hoped to quench my spiritual thirst. But I could never find a drop of water to quench the thirst of my heart. I was dying of thirst. When my spiritual eyes were opened, I saw the rivers of living water flowing from his pierced side. I drank of it and was satisfied. Thirst was no more.

Sadhu Sundar Singh

His are the thousand sparkling rills
　　That from a thousand fountains burst,
And fill with music all the hills:
　　And yet he saith, 'I thirst.'

O love most patient, give me grace;
　　Make all my soul athirst for thee:
That parched dry lip, that fading face,
　　That thirst, were all for me.

Mrs C. F. Alexander

Blessed Jesus, my Lord and my Master, who was pleased to thirst for our souls, grant that we may not be satisfied with the pleasures of this lower life, but ever thirst for the salvation of the souls thou didst die to save, and above all to thirst for thee.

Bishop Edward King

*

Lord Jesus, revealing true humanity in bodily need and true divinity through infinite love, may I always thirst for holiness in this world and by grace drink the water that rises up to eternal life.

I thirst for the water of life.

Good Friday

The Final Healing
John 19:30

When he had received the wine, he said, 'It is finished.' Then he bowed his head and gave up his spirit.

❖

It is finished. The human life that began in Bethlehem has run its course. Or rather, the long alienation of the human race from God, which began however and whenever the rebellious will was asserted against the Creator, has been set right. For these last words of Jesus on the Cross do not convey finality, a full stop that marks the end of a phase in history. The sense of the Greek word in the Gospel is rather, 'It is accomplished' – 'It has been achieved' – the statement of something done and yet continuing in its effect. Our Lord has accomplished the greatest of his healing miracles. Until the end of the world, for all who turn to him in faith, there will be spiritual light for those who walk in darkness; confident steps for those who have been limping their way through life; freedom for those paralysed by fear and anxiety; cleansing for those soiled by sin. It is a cry not of defeat but of the ultimate victory.

Yet even while we know the triumph of life over death, on this day we are right to mourn as we contemplate the terrible price of that victory. In the traditional hymns and prayers and readings that mark this day as the most solemn in the year, we suffer in our little way because such immeasurable love has suffered to bring us salvation. There have been so many deaths before and after this death on Calvary. Many, like Jesus, have died young, cut down when life seemed to be approaching fulfilment. Many, like Jesus, have died innocent, victims of power abused and hostility turned to hatred. Many, like Jesus, have died in great pain, tormented by violence or long illness. But none has died like Jesus, drawing the whole world into the love of outstretched arms.

◈

R edemption flashed through the hour of darkness,
blood cleansed the vile deeds of those who caused blood to be shed:
the betrayal, the denial, the false accusations, the cruelty,
the judgement that feared the power of Caesar above mercy.
It is finished, and we can only wonder and adore.

'It is finished.' The bridge, as it were, between heaven and earth is completed; Jacob's ladder is set up, and there is now a way from earth to heaven, and the poorest, and the most unlearned, and the youngest, the wayfaring man, may go on this way if they will and need not err. This was the joy of 'It is finished'.

Bishop Edward King

In the Cross, and Him who hung upon it, all things meet; all things subserve it, all things need it. It is their centre and their interpretation. For He was lifted up upon it, that He might draw all men and all things unto Him.

J. H. Newman

Ah, my dear Lord! what couldst thou spy
In this impure, rebellious clay,
That made thee thus resolve to die
For those that kill thee every day?

O what strange wonders could thee move
To slight thy precious blood and breath?
Sure it was Love, my Lord; for Love
Is only stronger far than death!

Henry Vaughan

Here, dying for the world, the world's life hung,
Laving a world's sin in that deathly tide;
The downbent head raised earth above the stars;
O timeless wonder! Life, because One died.

Alcuin of York

*

Hear us, O merciful Lord Jesus Christ, and remember now the hour in which thou didst commend thy blessed spirit into the hands of thy heavenly Father; and so assist us by this thy most precious death, that, being dead unto the world, we may live only unto thee; and that, at the hour of our departing from this mortal life, we may be received into thine everlasting kingdom, there to reign with thee, world without end.

Bishop John Cosin

Christ died that I might live.

Easter Eve

Day of Repose
John 19:38–42

Joseph of Arimathea, who was a disciple of Jesus, though a secret one because of his fear of the Jews, asked Pilate to let him take away the body of Jesus. Pilate gave him permission; so he came and removed his body. Nicodemus, who had at first come to Jesus by night, also came, bringing a mixture of myrrh and aloes, weighing about a hundred pounds. They took the body of Jesus and wrapped it with the spices in linen cloths, according to the burial custom of the Jews. Now there was a garden in the place where he was crucified, and in the garden there was a new tomb in which no one had ever been laid. And so, because it was the Jewish day of Preparation, and the tomb was nearby, they laid Jesus there.

❖

It is finished. The sacred body that began human life in a manger is laid in a hastily borrowed tomb. The myrrh brought by the Magi is the only gift that is needed, now that the gold of kingship and the incense of priesthood seem to have been taken away. Friends who feared to acknowledge Jesus as Lord while he lived now tend him in death.

The struggle is over. Vengeance for the disquieting of established lives has been taken, the menace to authority has been destroyed; there is no threat in a dead body.

Between the agony and the triumph, there is rest. On this day the Church rests and waits. We share the seventh day, the day of God's rest from creation, before the first day of creation newly created. Today there is neither the psalm of dereliction nor the hymn of triumph, only the silence of repose and waiting.

We have tried to share with the disciples and friends of Jesus, and especially with his Mother, the sad horror of his Passion. We have tried to stand at the foot of the Cross and hold out our hands to his pain. Today we cannot truly feel with them, because we know the end of the story. They are desolate, kept by the Sabbath laws from giving the last service to the body of their beloved Master. They are restless, torn by despair and forced inactivity. We can rest after the emotion of the last few days, and in expectation of the morrow.

Rest today. Be quiet and contented. Thank God for the gift of Lent, its challenges and its opportunities. Feel no pride in anything you have done, no guilt in anything you have failed to do. You have opened yourself to hear his word and do his will and it is enough. He accepts the failures in his mercy and gives the successes by his grace.

O Lord, calm the waves of this heart, calm its tempests. Calm thyself, O my soul, so that the divine can act in thee. Calm thyself, O my soul, so that God is able to repose in thee, so that his peace may cover thee. Yes, Father in heaven, often have we found that the world cannot give us peace. O but make us feel that thou art able to give peace; let us know the truth of thy promise that the whole world may not be able to take away thy peace.

Soren Kierkegaard

O Lord Jesus Christ, Son of the living God, who at the evening hour didst rest in the sepulchre, and didst thereby sanctify the grave to be a bed of hope for thy people: make us so to abound in sorrow for our sins, which were the cause of thy Passion, that when our bodies lie in the dust, our souls may live with thee; who livest and reigneth with the Father and the Holy Spirit, one God, world without end.

Compline Prayer

*

Gracious God, my guide and my strength in the forty days of this Lent, grant that the love of the Risen Christ may confirm all that has been achieved, pardon what has been left undone, and bring me day by day nearer to the eternal life promised to all who trust in him.

Christ has died
Christ is risen
Christ will come again.